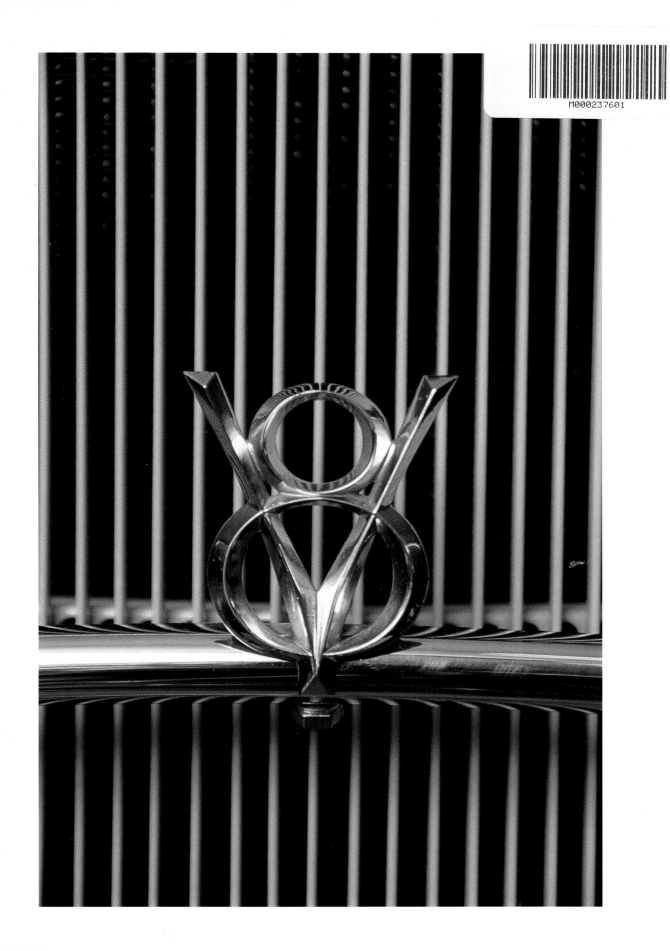

FORD `32 DEUCE
HOT RODS & HIBOYS

Timothy Remus

Motorbooks International
Publishers & Wholesalers

First published in 1991 by Motorbooks International Publishers & Wholesalers, PO Box 2, 729 Prospect Avenue, Osceola, WI 54020 USA

The information in this book is true and complete to the best of our knowledge. All recommendations are made without any guarantee on the part of the author or publisher, who also disclaim any liability incurred in connection with the use of this data or specific details

We recognize that some words, model names and designations, for example, mentioned herein are the property of the trademark holder. We use them for identification purposes only. This is not an official publication

Motorbooks International books are also available at discounts in bulk quantity for industrial or sales-promotional use. For details write to Special Sales Manager at the Publisher's address

Library of Congress Cataloging-in-Publication Data
Remus, Timothy.
    Ford '32 Deuce hot rods & hiboys / Timothy Remus.
        p.   cm.
    Includes index.
    ISBN 0-87938-542-1
    1. Hot rods.   2. Ford automobile—Customizing.   I. Title. II. Title: Ford thirty-two Deuce hot rods and hiboys.
TL236.3.R46 1991
629.228—dc20   91-14144

Printed and bound in Hong Kong

On the front cover: *The home-built Deuce hot rod powered by a 354 ci Chrysler Hemi and constructed by Mickey Cox.*

On the frontispiece: *Ford V-8 grille detail from Gene Hetland's restored Deuce.*

On the title page: *The Deuce roadster owned by Roger Ward.*

On the back cover: *An American tradition: Lon Lewis' '32 coupe hot rod at the local root beer stand.*

Contents

Acknowledgments

Though it might seem like a solitary occupation, writing a book like this requires help and guidance from a number of people.

First I must thank the Deuce owners. Sure, they all want their car to appear in a book—but most of them went to considerable lengths to accommodate me and my camera. For some owners it was simply a matter of taking time out of their day and then moving the car this way and that. For others, there was more than just moving the car. Dan Hix spent the morning running water down his driveway with a garden hose. Ken Fenical gave up his morning so I could photograph both of the cars he built. Barry Larson jacked up his phaeton and found some nice, neat stands to set the front tires on. Lon Lewis drove his coupe to the drive-in, moved it at least a hundred times—and worried all the while that the battery would go dead because I wanted the lights on and the motor off. To them and all the others, I say thanks.

Then there's Gary Meddors, the man responsible for those great Goodguys events. Gary gave me the run of his Indy event and provided some good advice to boot. Don Cain from Kansas City was kind enough to introduce me to many of the members of the Deuce club so I could photograph their cars.

I have to thank Dean Batchelor for providing some great old photos of early Deuces. The timely pictures in the first chapter are Dean's, in fact one of the drivers pictured *is* Dean.

And of course there's Steve Hendrickson, well-known editor of that great street-rodding magazine, *Rodder's Digest*. When it comes to the English language and all the many rules that govern its use, Steve is the most persnickety, inflexible guy I've ever known—and for this I am eternally grateful.

As I prepare to turn in my third book to Motorbooks, I realize that I've come a long way with this hobby of photography I picked up some fifteen years ago. Maybe it's true that we *can* get anything we want if we just want it badly enough. Final thanks should go to my dad, Frank Remus, long gone now. I have to thank Frank not for any specific skill, but rather for encouraging me in my endeavors (no matter how crazy they must have seemed) and for never telling me there was something I *couldn't* do.

Introduction

When I took the assignment from Motorbooks to create a book about 1932 Fords, it seemed a tall order. I mean, there are so many of these lovely cars, how was I to pick the "right" ones? What if I missed some anecdote of history or misstated some well-known fact?

Although my position with *Midwest Rod & Machine* and later, *Rodder's Digest*, gave me some background, I wasn't sure that I really knew enough about Deuces to write a book.

Thus I became a student of the '32 Ford. Even before the actual writing and photography began, I would walk the grounds of each event with my eye out for Deuces. When I found one, I looked it over and compared it mentally to the others at that event. I read everything I could find about Deuces, including Tony Thacker's fine book, *'32 Ford: The Deuce* (Osprey).

All in all, I learned a lot. I learned that the Deuce was a special car right from its inception. A car that truly broke away from those before it. A vehicle that set new standards for personal transportation. A rare combination of outstanding power and great looks. The '55 Chevy of its day, the Deuce soon became the only car to own. It was a good-looking, fast ride, one that could easily be modified to produce more power.

After looking at hundreds of Deuces, I began to pick the cars to feature in this book. I looked first for quality. I wanted each car to represent a high standard of workmanship. A car built—whether by Boyd Coddington or Joe Smith—to the highest possible standards.

Next, I looked for variety because there are so many different kinds of Deuces. There are early cars and late cars, high-tech rods and retro rods, simple hot rods and sophisticated street rods. I tried to find a wide array of cars, from early roadsters with flathead power to fastback designs that go beyond high tech.

I assume most readers are already fans of the '32 Ford, though perhaps this book will deepen your appreciation for the Deuce. What I hope comes through to you is an appreciation for both the original Ford design and the modified cars that have been built based on that design—whether or not you agree with everything the owner did. The strength of street rodding and hot rodding lies in innovation, having the guts to do something different and hopefully better. I further hope that this book will encourage individuals looking for ideas to apply to their own projects.

In writing about each car, I tried to include the owner or builder in the story. Often, the reason for building the car is nearly as important as the construction details of the car itself. Readers should understand that each car was first conceived and then constructed; that each car is the end result of a lengthy process requiring the skill and labor of a number of individuals.

The book is arranged in a kind of evolutionary order. The stock Deuces and the early cars help to give an appreciation for the roots of street rodding. The most futuristic cars provide—I hope—an inspiration to all of us by proving that new designs require only new thinking.

A Deuce that stirs the soul. Doug Wamsher's hot rod coupe is powered by a towering 350 ci Chevrolet small-block, topped with two Holley carbs and a GMC-Dyers Blower.

Deuces Forever

A Design That Never Got Old

Why the Deuce? Why among all the cars and all the models manufactured since the turn of the century has the 1932 Ford been such a hit with nearly everyone? What is the unique mix of elements that has kept this one car near the top of the popularity charts for almost sixty years?

Perhaps the answer lies in the car's new V-8—the first mass-produced V-8. The legendary Flathead. Others would say no, the popularity of the Deuce lies in its great looks. The lines that flow so nicely from grille shell to gas tank.

Like so many other things, the popularity of the Deuce has no simple answer. In searching for the correct answer it might be instructive to make a short study of the Deuce, its development and history.

Development of a Classic

It seems hard to believe now, but there almost wasn't a Deuce at all. At least not in the sense that the 1932 Ford was very different from the Model A that preceded it. In September of 1931 plans and drawings were well along for the 1932 Fords, known as the Model B. Production supervisors had begun to order the tooling that would be necessary to produce the next year's car.

That car was slated to be an updated Model A with more modern styling, a slightly longer wheelbase and an improved four-cylinder engine. There were no plans for a V-8.

The first Model Bs came off the assembly line in December of 1931 with their new styling and four-cylinder engines. Suddenly, on December 7, Henry Ford brought the entire assembly plant to a halt and sent most of the workers home. While Henry would keep it secret as long as possible, he had decided—after consulting with his son Edsel—to produce a new, V-8 engine with a one-piece block.

No one knows for sure why Henry decided to build a V-8 or why he waited so long to make the decision. Chevrolet and Plymouth, his key competitors, both offered six-cylinder engines in the same price range as Henry's fours. Cars were becoming larger and more sophisticated as well. More power was needed to pull the larger cars at higher speeds.

Prior to 1932 the only V-8s offered to American car owners were those found in the larger and much more expensive cars like Lincoln and Cadillac. Built in low volume, these engines utilized two- or three-piece engine blocks. The challenge to Henry and his engineers was twofold. Not only did they need to produce the first mass-produced V-8—they also would have to do it efficiently so the price of the finished car would not be too high.

Early '32 Ford hot rodders on their way home from Lake Tahoe in 1947. Right, original advertising copy from a Ford brochure for 1932. Note the 75 mph claim, definitely high speed for 1932.

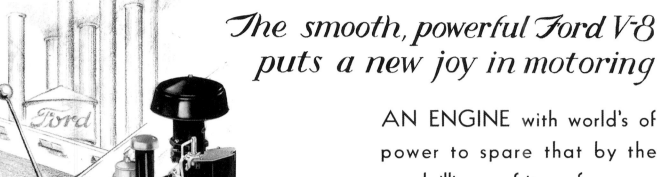
The idea of a V-8 design had existed since the turn of the century, though there were many problems. In 1923 Cadillac developed the first counterweighted V-8 crankshaft, making a smooth-running V-8 a real possibility. Henry had wanted to produce a one-piece V-8 engine for years. In fact, secret developmental engines were built and tested starting in 1928.

The early engines ran rough and they ran hot. Henry placed specific parameters on the engine's design. Simplicity was paramount. Henry wanted a V-8 with a one-piece block that would require no water pump, no fuel pump and not even an oil pump. He insisted that the ignition be contained in one housing, driven off the camshaft at the front of the engine. He further insisted that the exhaust passages run through the block, between the cylinders, instead of exiting the block at the top like some of the other Flathead V-8 designs.

The teething problems encountered with the early test-mule engines were many. The unique self-feeding carburetor worked, but only under ideal conditions and eventually a fuel pump was added. Overheating problems forced the Ford engineers to use water pumps, though the always frugal Henry directed that Model A pumps be used, one on each side. An oil pump was added to the design after test engines run in modified Model A cars continued to burn out bearings.

The list of problems suffered by the early Flathead V-8s were many, though the biggest single problem Henry had to overcome was the successful

August 13, 1939, Eddie Meyer streaks across Rosamond dry lake in his Deuce roadster. Eddie's time was 121.62 mph. He was one of the early racers who went on to produce hop-up parts for the Flathead V-8.
Dean Batchelor

casting of his one-piece block. The first production blocks were cast on March 14, 1932. Of that first production batch not one block passed inspection.

The V–8 block was a much more complex piece to cast than the old four-cylinder block. Cores used in casting (pieces having the shapes of cylinders or water jackets; places molten metal is not wanted) numbered forty-three for the V–8 and only eleven for the four-cylinder. The exhaust passages that passed through the block also passed through the water jacket. Successful casting of the V–8 meant precise placement of the cores. Thus the early engines were doomed, as the cores would shift during the pouring and cooling process.

Finally, the foundry tried refractory paste to hold the cores in place while the blocks were cast. The refractory paste solved the problem and by late March of 1932, more than 100 engines were being assembled per day.

Those first V–8 engines used a bore of 3⅛₆ in. and a stroke of 3¾ in. for a total displacement of 221

Dean Batchelor poses in his Deuce roadster at El Mirage dry lake, 1948. By this time the Deuce roadster had become the single most common car seen at the lakes. Dean Batchelor

Fancier than most, Duane Spencer's Deuce roadster features a Du Vall windshield and smooth hood sides. Leaning on the car is George Hill who went on to pilot the Hill-Davis streamliner at Bonneville. Dean Batchelor

A modern interpretation of a classic car. Harry and Vicki Ruthrauff of Coldwater, Michigan, have built a Deuce roadster with a Chrysler Hemi for power. Note the wire wheels, nerf bars, external hinges and door handles, and stock grille shell—all hallmarks of the early Deuce hot rods. Rodder's Digest

An early Hot Rod magazine cover car, Dick Scritchfield sits in his very clean Deuce Roadster. The car has a custom, three-piece hood, tube shocks and trick exhaust with lakes plugs. Dean Batchelor

ci. Cast-iron, twenty-one-stud heads gave a compression ratio of 5.5:1. An unusual valve design included a flared end that rode directly on the cam. The best machines are the simple ones—no lifters meant fewer pieces and a lighter valvetrain. The flared end on the lower end of the valve required a two-piece valve guide, held in the block by clips.

Flatheads built in 1932 were equipped with a single-barrel, Detroit Lubricator carburetor mounted on a cast-aluminum, single-plane manifold.

The first cars were introduced on March 31, 1932. Edsel Ford worried that the new V–8—an engine that had gone from early prototype to full production in less than four months—would give

Typical 1940s Hiboy roadster, Dean Batchelor's Deuce sits in front of Alex Xydia's southern California speed shop. Dean Batchelor

trouble to the first buyers. Edsel was right. Ford Motor Company replaced thousands of early ignition coils and did enormous numbers of free piston and ring jobs to cure problems of heavy oil burning.

Yet, with Henry Ford's persistence and the enormous resources of Ford Motor Company, the new "V-8 cylinder" 1932 Ford was launched. It's estimated that more than five million people crowded into the Ford showrooms across the country on March 31 to see the new car.

Seeing was one thing, but buying was another. The Depression was still on and sales were slow to build. Even people with enough cash to buy a new Ford were slow to part with their hard-earned dollars. The new '32 Ford was quite a car, however. The 65 hp in a light car provided for dramatic acceleration. Henry realized right away that the car would sell itself if the sales force could only get people to test drive the car. The new sales slogan for the Ford Motor Company became "Driving means buying."

Sales records for 1932 put production figures at 256,867. Of this total approximately two thirds of the cars were equipped with the new V-8.

Deuce Flathead Becomes The Hot Rod of Choice

Though the new Deuce was fast and powerful it was some years before the hot rodders of the day would accept the new engine. During the 1930s the vehicle of choice for a young man was usually a Model A roadster with a modified four-cylinder engine. High-compression heads from companies like Winfield or full overhead-valve conversions from Riley were combined with two-carb intake manifolds. Stripped of fenders and running boards but mounted with a set of wire wheels, these Model As were the hot ticket in their day.

By the late 1930s the young men building hot cars came to realize that a Deuce roadster could be had for only a bit more than a Model A. Right off, the Deuce had a number of advantages: The V-8 offered more potential for speed than all but the most exotic four-cylinder engines. It didn't hurt that later, and larger, Flatheads would drop into a Deuce frame without any modification. The Deuce was also larger inside than the earlier cars and thus made a better daily driver.

The list goes on and on. While Model A fenders and running boards could be stripped off easily for racing, the splash aprons wrapped up and over the frame. On Deuces the running boards attached directly to the frame with no splash aprons. Removal of the Deuce fenders and running boards was easy and made an instant "Hiboy." A Deuce roadster body sitting on top of the frame—with the nice flare at the bottom of the frame rail—looked great and became the standard hot machine.

Acceptance of the Flathead and the growing popularity of the Deuce provided a good market for speed equipment. Racers like Eddie Meyer and Vic Edelbrock began producing high-compression heads and two-carb manifolds. Soon all the record-holding cars at the California dry lakes were Deuce roadsters with full-house Flatheads.

World War II interrupted most of this activity, as the nation's young men went off to war. In 1945 and 1946, however, many of those young men came home through California and many stayed. Action at the dry lakes took up where it left off and soon a whole new sport was born—drag racing.

The Deuce Evolves to Street Rod

Through it all, from the first issue of *Hot Rod* magazine in 1948 to the creation of street rodding in the late 1960s, there have been 1932 Fords. The first ones were Hiboy roadsters. As the years went by, the young men now known as hot rodders began to appreciate the coupe body, preferably the three-window design. In time nearly all the Deuce bodystyles came to be desirable hot rod material.

Deuces have been chopped, channeled and sectioned. Powerplants ranging from the Flathead to the Mopar Hemi, from the original Model B four-cylinder to the rare sohc Ford V-8 have been placed between those legendary Deuce rails. The popularity of the Deuce keeps a number of firms producing everything from fiberglass bodies and grille shells to Deuce rails and complete frames.

Deuces have been popular for so long that current builders have a choice: To make their Deuce look new and high-tech, or old and original like the first Deuces that ran the lakes and the streets forty and fifty years ago.

Anyone who doubts the ability of individuals to create their own unique Deuce designs hasn't seen the work of Thom Taylor as interpreted by Ken Fenical, owner of Posies street rod shop.

In short, the Deuce, with its first-ever mass-produced V-8, was one of the fastest stock cars of 1932. When hot rodders discovered the Deuce in the late 1930s it just got faster and more popular. Today, nearly sixty years later, the '32 Ford is as popular as ever—and there's no end in sight.

Seen at a recent show, this Deuce coupe isn't so different from those seen forty years ago. Note the louvered hood, chopped top and hairpin radius rods. Rodder's Digest

The Deuce That Henry Built

As Seen Then—and Now

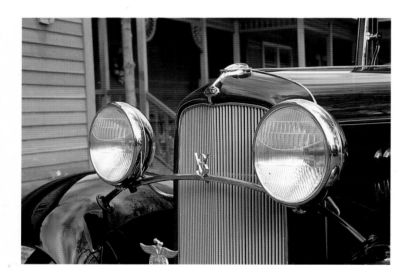

Before going on to examine the Deuce as a hot rod or street rod, it might be instructive to examine the Deuce as a car. What did Henry Ford create? What was this wonderful V-8 car that he unleashed on the world in March of 1932?

The two cars pictured here are intended to help answer that question. Both cars belong to Gene Hetland of Minneapolis, a collector of '32 Fords. His basement is filled with beautiful finished cars and a substantial collection of memorabilia. Gene discovered the Deuce as a hot rodder, though he soon became a restorer of stock '32 Fords.

The '32 Fords that we see on the street these days are nearly always modified versions of Henry's creation—roadsters and coupes with Chevrolet engines and alloy wheels. We often forget that the '32 Ford was offered in fourteen bodystyles, from standard roadsters selling for $430 to deluxe convertible sedans for $650.

What follows is a look at two of the Ford models, the relatively common roadster and the rare convertible sedan, sometimes known as the B-400. Perhaps an examination of these two cars can help us to understand where the Deuce started and where it's going.

Convertible Sedan

The year 1932 was the last for the convertible sedan. Though it had been offered as part of the Model A line, sales in 1932 were disappointing with a total of less than 1,000. If roadsters were relatively inexpensive and plentiful, the B-400 was both expensive and uncommon.

Though Gene's convertible sedan looks to be much larger than the accompanying roadster, both ride on the same frame and the same 106 in. wheelbase. The stock Ford frame is a simple ladder design with three cross-members. The frame reflects Henry's belief that a good design should be both light and simple.

The suspension at either end of this B-400 follows the same theory as the frame. At the front, a single, transverse leaf spring suspends the car. The axle itself is held in position by the spring and the wishbone, mounted to either side of the axle and pivoting at a single point at the central cross-member.

The rear suspension also utilizes only one spring, mounted buggy style across the frame. Both front and rear axles use lever-action, hydraulic shock absorbers—quite an improvement over the friction shocks commonly used during the period.

By today's standards this stock B-400 looks tall and elegant. The top of the Ford line for 1932, fewer than 1,000 of these convertible sedans were sold and the model was not offered in 1933. Though it looks to be a much larger car than a roadster or coupe, the B-400 rides on the same basic chassis as the roadster.

With its two-tone paint and chrome-plated spare-tire cover this B-400 looks more like a Lincoln than a lowly Ford. In 1932, a convertible sedan equipped with the new Flathead V-8 cost $650, while a V-8 roadster cost only $460.

Gene's B-400 is completely stock, right down to its mechanical brakes. He reports that the brakes actually work pretty well, as long as the owner is careful to keep all the linkages adjusted.

Externally this B-400 differs dramatically from its roadster sibling. The two-tone paint, chrome windshield frame and fabric top with its unique lines give this car a certain elegance more befitting a

Interior of the stock roadster looks simple. No digital displays, the instrument cluster holds only an ammeter, fuel gauge and speedometer. The two small knobs are for the throttle and light switch; the choke knob is hidden by the steering wheel. The machined or turned mounting panel provides a nice texture.

Lincoln than a Ford. The B-400 was offered in only one trim level: deluxe. Deluxe trim included the cowl lights and a higher grade of interior finishing. Gene's B-400 has the leather-covered seats—the most expensive of the trim options—with matching brown carpets and door panels. Mounted on the steering column is a seldom-seen option, a control head for the AM radio.

Deluxe Roadster

The other car seen here is a bone-stock roadster. With its rakish lines and fabric top it's easy to understand how the '32 Ford became the nation's favorite hot rod.

The roadster shows off the lines and style of the Deuce to good effect. As Gene says: "Everything on

*The first Deuces to be hot rodded were the roadsters.
Looking at this stock roadster it's not hard to understand
why—even in stock trim the car has a certain sporty look.
The rounded grille shell, the relatively long hood and
cowl and the flowing lines of the fenders all combine to
give a Deuce roadster the right stuff.*

a Deuce has its place, everything fits, the design
really flows from the front to the back." At the front,
the large-diameter headlights stand on the graceful
support rod with its wonderful V–8 logo. Behind the
headlights is one of the most beautiful grille shells
ever designed. The hood seems rather long, flowing
gracefully back to the cowl. It's interesting to note
that the wheelbase of the Deuce is 3 in. longer than
the Model A. Looking at the roadster it's easy to
assume that most of that extra length went into the
hood.

The folding, stainless windshield stanchions
make it possible to lay the windshield across the
cowl like an early safari car. Across the top of the
door the three snaps allow the owner to snap on side
curtains in inclement weather. Though the
differences are subtle, the rear half of the body
behind the door opening is different from a Model A.
The rear deck of the Deuce is higher, allowing a
smoother sweep down to the rear bumper. Mounted
just ahead of the rear bumper is the twelve-gallon
gas tank. Perhaps not a location Ralph Nader would
approve, the rear tank location was far superior to
the cowl tank used in the preceding Model A.

*Interior of the convertible sedan shows top-of-the-line
trim for 1932. Seats are covered in leather, carpet is wool.
Note the head for the AM radio, a rare option.*

Under the hood of Gene's roadster is a well-tuned example of Henry's first Flathead. The bore of 3¹⁄₁₆ in. and stroke of 3¾ in. provides a displacement of 221 ci. A compression ratio of 5.5:1 and a single-barrel carburetor net a total of 65 hp. That may not seem like much today, but in 1932, when placed in one of Henry's light roadster bodies, sixty-five horses was significant.

Later Flatheads would sport a series of improvements: A two-barrel carburetor, better bearings for the crankshaft, relocated water pumps and more displacement. The thing that didn't change was the location of the holes used to bolt on the front motor mounts. What this meant was that later Flatheads, from 1933 to 1953, would drop right into a Deuce frame for an almost instant hot rod.

What did Henry Ford create? He created more than just a light, powerful and durable car. The car he offered to the American public was truly a revolutionary design. Looking at these two stock examples of the breed, it becomes easy to see just how revolutionary the design was. Truly great designs don't come along often, and when they do, they exhibit a certain staying power, somehow never becoming old or dated.

The 1932 Ford is just that—a great automotive design. One that still looks fresh almost sixty years after its creation. A car that men and women have been rebuilding and modifying since it was new. A design where, as Gene says, "Everything turned out just right."

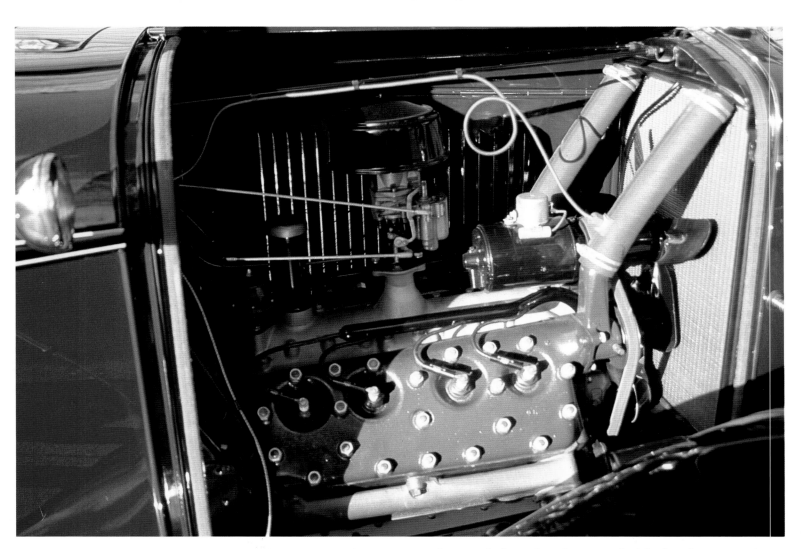

The heart of the 1932 Ford was Henry's new engine, the first mass-produced V-8. With a bore of 3¹⁄₁₆ in. and a stroke of 3¾ in., the Flathead displaced 221 ci. Equipped with a single-barrel carburetor the Flathead was rated at 65 hp and 142 lb-ft of torque—this was the factory hot rod of its day.

Top Dog

Good Breeding Pays Off

The fact that '32 Fords have been near the top of the most desirable hot rod heap almost since their creation means that some of today's cars have long, complicated histories. If John Holland's Deuce roadster were a Dalmatian, he could point proudly to its pedigree—all the prize-winning animals that contributed their genes to create what turned out to be a top dog.

The original sire of John's roadster was a Fordor Deuce with low miles that was given by an uncle in South Dakota to his nephew in Iowa. The nephew promptly ripped off the body with all the doors and replaced it with a three-window-coupe body. At the same time he installed a later-model Flatty, '39 Ford three-speed tranny and a later rear-axle assembly (still a torque-tube style) with juice brakes. This second-generation transformation occurred in about 1957.

Thirteen years later, the car had once again been reduced to a bare frame with suspension and grille shell. Russel Post was the breeder of the next generation. Russel bought the pile of Deuce bones (Ford DNA molecules, if you will) and drug them back to his place in the small town of Alta, Iowa. Russel had, in his words, "Been gathering parts for an early fifties style rod of some type."

Starting fresh, Russel installed a Flathead from a 1942 truck. This V-8 started out as Henry's 90 hp Flatty, with significant additions by the new owner. Some of the bits and pieces Russel had been collecting included a twin-carb Weiand intake manifold, two of the legendary Stromberg 97 carbs and a pair of Fenton heads. A Ford truck clutch was used to take the power to the same '39 transmission and early-style rear end.

The body and the various bits and pieces that Russel used to round out the car are an ingenious mix of old and new. The roadster body, the one that looks like such a "genny," is a glass body from Gibbon. The headlights are of indeterminate origin. Russel says: "The headlight stands are the ends off a Model A headlight bar that were heated and bent to suit. The headlights are of unknown make, I found them at a local junkyard in the late 1970s—they might be off an old tractor."

Russel eventually sold the car, and a series of owners contributed to the car's evolution. The current owner, John Holland of Rogers, Minnesota, bought the car about one year ago. At that time, it was the same roadster body on the same, original Deuce rails. The same 1942 truck Flathead sat under the hood, connected to that early Ford drivetrain with the torque-tube-style rear end.

John Holland's roadster carries all the right equipment for an early Hiboy hot rod: Flathead, original grille shell and solid wheels with big and little tires. Though the front suspension is a four-bar, the rear suspension is early Ford complete with single leaf spring and torque-tube drive.

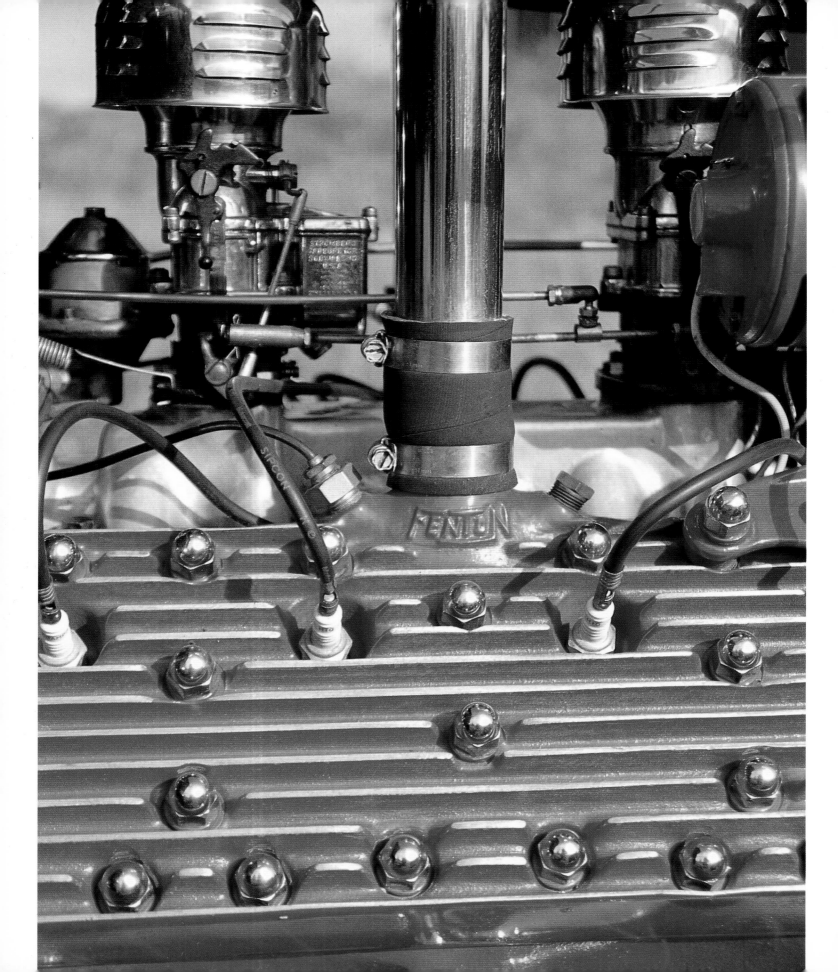

This Flathead V-8 started out in a 1942 Ford truck. Early speed equipment includes Fenton heads, Weiand two-carb intake manifold and two Stromberg carburetors.

Changes to the car included the fabric top, turn signals and windshield wiper. In front, the old split wishbone had been replaced with a more modern four-bar suspension, and the early Ford juice brakes had been set aside in favor of aftermarket disc brakes.

John wanted a hot rod he could drive. The roadster was a nice car in need of a little extra maintenance. He simply went through the car from one end to the other. A good tune-up was at the top of the list, starting with a disassembly of the leaky

The body and the various bits and pieces that Russel used to round out the car are an ingenious mix of old and new

Strombergs. After taking them all apart, the body castings were planed flat and a pair of rebuild kits were installed. In the interest of dependability, the 6 volt electrics were converted to 12 volt and an

Next page
This Hiboy started out as a Fordor and spent a number of years as a coupe before the final transformation to roadster status.

Super Bell axle and linkage have received the chrome treatment. Steering is early style, with the drag link running along the frame rail on the left side.

Though the four-bar suspension and disc brakes seem too modern, they make the car much safer and more driveable.

electric cooling fan was added to supplement the belt-driven fan.

When it was finished, John and his sons teamed up with seven other street rodders for a trip to Columbus, Ohio, and the Nationals. Some of his friends were skeptical when they saw the roadster with its Flathead power. They envisioned long delays along the freeway while John made repairs to that "undependable old Flathead." John reports that the trip came off without a hitch. The only members of their little caravan who had any car trouble were

The nephew promptly ripped off the body with all the doors and replaced it with a three-window-coupe body

some of the guys with those small-block-powered cars.

Red and black, John's Flathead-powered Hiboy with the steel wheels takes us back to the early days of hot rods. Through at least two generations, with a lot of input to improve the breed, the tinkering has left us a surprisingly original Deuce roadster. It was a hot rod in 1957; some would call it a street rod today. The exact term doesn't really matter—John's old Deuce roadster has been a cool car for thirty-five years now, with at least another thirty-five to go.

The dash layout is simple and close to stock. Large chrome shift knob connects to a '39 Merc three-speed transmission. Wood-rim steering wheel with wire spokes seems period-correct. Note the V-8 logo.

The Invincible Olds Is Born Again

Some Hot Rods Are More Invincible than Others

Older members of the street rod and hot rod fraternity will remember a particularly fast Deuce coupe known as the *Invincible Olds*. Run by the Hix brothers of Pittsburg, Kansas, the car took home many a trophy from the drag strip during the late 1950s and early 1960s. Originally powered by a Flathead, the car was eventually powered by a 371 ci blown Olds V-8. Dan Hix, the man who bought the car in 1954, sold it in 1969. That might be the end of the story, except that he bought back the car some ten years ago and fully restored it.

Dan's story of how he bought and built the old Deuce during the mid 1950s is more than just a story about a boy and his car. Between the lines of Dan's story are images from Main Street America and all the young men who grew up there. As Dan tells it, the story goes like this:

"I got the car in 1954 during high school. I had a pretty nice '39 Merc convertible. I traded this '39 Merc convertible for the coupe. The Merc had a full-race Flathead in it. So I took out the Flathead and we traded cars—minus the engines. The '32 I bought didn't have any fenders, it was just a body, a frame, a rear end and a front end.

"I was about 16 or 17 at the time. I took it home and after putting the engine in I promptly took the body off the frame. I knew I was going to channel that sucker. . . . I took the mattress off my bed, took it out in the yard, covered it with carboard and rolled the body off onto the mattress. Then I cut the floor out of it. Next, I took the floor over to a set of sawhorses and welded some four inch strips of metal all the way around the edges. Then I took the floor back over and slid it back up inside of the body, which was lying on its side, and welded the floor back into the body.

"I put the body back on the frame and it was channeled—which was kind of unusual in those days—cause everyone would just cut the floor out with a torch and then let the body fall down and then just bolt the body right to the side rails of the frame. The way I did it the car still used the original body mounting bolts.

"So then I ran around with this Flathead-powered, channeled car for a couple of years. In

Channeled coupe was the Invincible Olds, an Olds-powered terror of the drag strips during the fifties and sixties. Twenty-five years of wear and tear became invisible after a complete restoration. Moonroof was added during the recent renovation.

The wheels are Halibrands. Dan Hix's coupe is channeled 4 in. and chopped 1¼ in.—providing a nice low stance without putting the chassis in the weeds. Note the period-correct external door handles and hinges.

Next page
Gas tank has been moved and replaced by a neat rolled pan and frenched license plate. Small chrome grille below the license plate is actually a third brakelight. Rear suspension is a four-bar; rear end is the venerable 9 in. Ford.

about 1956 I decided I wanted to go to the drags and I found out that I fit in an Altered class with no fenders. I didn't want to run Altered class, so I rounded me up some fenders. I found a Ford dealer who still had two brand new front fenders hanging in the rafters, I think I paid $25 for the pair.

"I found some Model A rear fenders, they were an inch or so wider than the '32 fenders, which was good cause I needed the wider fenders, but of course the body sat lower than stock so the tires rubbed on

"We had pistons all over the damn yard and folded up connecting rods and blown head gaskets. When we would screw out a spark plug there wouldn't be anything on the end of it."

Previous page
Restoration included fabrication of new rear fenders using two old fenders as a starting point. Fenders sit higher on the quarter panel because the car has been channeled.

the fenders. Well, I took the fenders back off and took a string from the middle of the axle and drew a curve on the body. And then I cut out that part of the quarter panel and then welded the fender into the body—crude, I mean it was really crude—and then I leaded it all up, it looked pretty good to me at the time. . . . I mean you're talking about an 18 or 19 year old guy.

"The first time I went to the drags was in 1957 and the coupe went as an A/Gas car. It had the Flathead in it, it turned 97 miles per hour in 14.10 seconds and I got a trophy. It was a strong Flathead, a big Flathead. Not long after that I decided I wanted to go faster and faster (I was really bitten by the drag race bug). My brother Clifford had a '49 Olds fastback with a real powerful 371 Olds engine in it. He left the Olds at home when he went into the service—so I took the engine out and put it in the coupe. By the time he got back we had a '32 Ford with an Olds engine in it.

"We were starting to become the Hix brothers by that time. One day we saw this thing sitting on

Dash layout is simple and uses round, analog gauges. Interior is all leather, stitched up by Don Kite from Kansas City, Missouri.

top of a motor, made it real powerful—a blower you know. So we went out and rounded up all these parts so we could have a blown engine. We got it running, but boy we fried lots of pieces. No one knew what the hell they were doing . . . we had pistons all over the damn yard and folded up connecting rods and blown head gaskets. When we would screw out a spark plug there wouldn't be anything on the end of it, just the case like someone had taken a cutting torch to the two electrodes. . . . It took us awhile but eventually we learned how to make it run.

"By late 1957 we had it running good. At the 1958 Nationals in Oklahoma City we had it wrapped up to take top time and the eliminator title. On the elimination run we ran out of gas, we had put this little bitty gas tank on it and we just barely got beat. . . . We did come back later during the Nationals and set top speed for our class at 113.35 miles per hour. Well, we kept on, improving the car each year, adding fuel injection and always getting the times lower and lower. Finally, by 1968 or 1969 we started running another car, a '32 Bantam with a big-block—the old Deuce just wasn't fast enough anymore . . . so I sold the car to a friend of mine who wanted to make it a street car again.

"And then about 10 years ago my wife Joan said, 'You ought to go get that old car back and fix it up' Well, the guy wouldn't sell it, we argued back and forth until finally I bought the car. When I got it back it was like the first time I bought it: I got just the body, fenders, frame and radiator shell. No motor and no transmission."

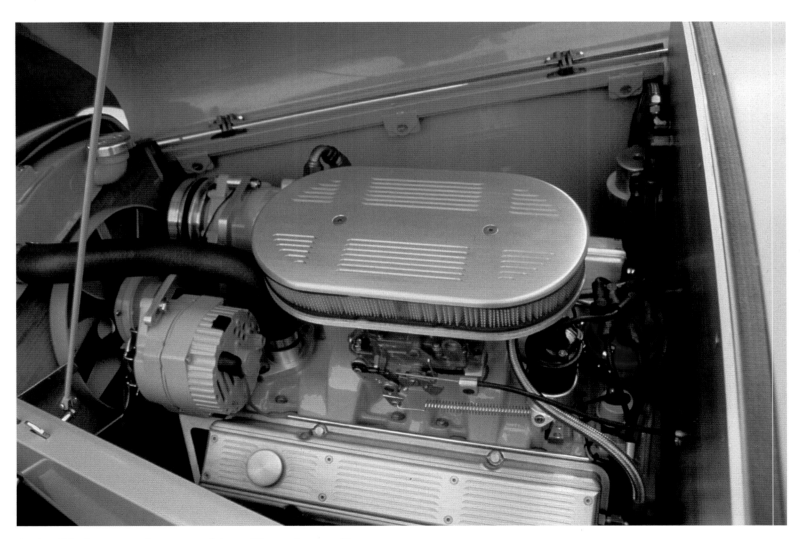

Invincible *is currently powered by a Chevrolet small-block V-8 with a four-barrel carburetor.*

Although the old Invincible *has been updated from earlier days, the front suspension retains the split wishbones and dropped I-beam axle.*

The rebirth of Dan's *Invincible Olds* started with a trip to Carriage Works to talk with Curt Cunningham. Curt has a reputation for good chassis and flawless metal work, and Dan (now tied up twelve hours a day with his own business) thought Curt would be the man to bring the Deuce coupe back to its former glory.

The first thing Curt did was pull the body off the frame and send it out to be boiled. What Curt and Dan found when the body came back almost convinced them to give up the project. Dan remembers: "When we got the body back it was just awful. You could see all the rash from all those years on the strip, the frame was all bowed and bent and you could see those hideous fenders I'd welded on years ago."

Curt started the restoration process by pulling off those fenders. The damage from the earlier cutting and welding was too extensive, so Curt welded in a new set of quarter panels. During their drag-racing days the Hix brothers went to nearly any lengths to lighten their car. Another challenge facing Curt as he tried to reassemble the car was the missing inner door skins and trunk lid. In both cases the inner panels had to be fabricated from scratch. As the body started to come together Peter Wietz, a craftsman visiting from New Zealand, became involved.

Peter made up a set of new rear fenders almost from scratch and went on to form the roll pan where the gas tank would normally be. Though the original car was unchopped, Dan had decided on a modest chop. Peter was given the nod, and the lid came down 1¼ in. At the same time, a sliding moonroof from a Ford Capri was installed.

The chassis under Dan's Deuce was assembled by Carriage Works using original Deuce rails and Carriage Works cross-members. At the front a traditional set of split wishbones and a single, buggy-style spring hold the axle in place.

At the rear, the original ladder bars were replaced with a modern four-bar system with coil-over shocks mounting a Ford 9 in. rear axle. A custom driveshaft ties the Ford rear end to a Turbo 400 transmission mated to a Chevy small-block. The Chevrolet engine was built by Dan, who explains:

"Even if I don't do all the work on my cars anymore, I always build the engines." The motor Dan built uses low-compression smogger pistons in conjunction with stock connecting rods and a stock crank. The 268 degree camshaft helps the engine breathe through the Carter four-barrel carb.

As the project started to come together Dan had to choose an upholstery shop. The man he chose is Don Kite from Kansas City, Missouri. Better known as an upholsterer of exclusive cars and aircraft, Don did the entire interior in black leather. The leather stretches across the seats and door panels without a wrinkle—even the speaker grilles have been integrated into the flawless and almost seamless interior.

The final massage of the body panels, the block sanding and the paint was done by Roger Ward of Ottawa, Kansas. The final paint, as applied by Roger, is Wisteria Lavender, the same '56 Lincoln hue originally used on the car.

After six long years, Dan Hix finally had his old Deuce back on the road—almost. It was all there and all bolted together, but the car still needed someone to go over it from end to end and make all the adjustments. Things like the collars on the coil-overs and the number of leafs in the front buggy spring and the way the driver's door closes and a thousand other little details. The person to take care of all those little things was Leon Holman from Kansas City. Leon made sure that everything worked, that the car rode and handled correctly and that all the details were completed.

The "new" Deuce coupe still carries the *Invincible* logo in the pinstriping. What else can you call a car that went from stocker to early hot rod to drag racer to street car to street rod? With more lives than an alley cat, Dan's Coupe is still rolling down the road more invincible than ever.

Dan Hix, the man who with his brother Clifford built and ran the Invincible Olds. Though he no longer drag races, Dan's garage houses another Deuce roadster and a Model A.

Hemi-Deuce

A Deuce from the "Home-Built" Company

The tech sheet for the Deuce belonging to Mickey Cox is a little different than most. Where it asks for engine type, the word Chevrolet doesn't appear anywhere. And when the same tech sheet asks for the manufacturer of the front and rear suspension, the manufacturer is listed as Home-Built. Home-Built, is this some new street rod manufacturing company? Let's see, according to the tech sheet they make front and rear four-bar suspensions, trick wheels in a variety of sizes, intake manifolds and even exhaust systems.

Perhaps it's not so surprising to find a street rodder with the skills to manufacture a large measure of his own car. It does, however, seem unusual to find a nonprofessional builder with such a wide variety of fabrication skills.

Mickey Cox learned his many home-building skills during the eighteen years he spent campaigning dragsters in the southern part of the country. He built frames for C, B and top alcohol dragsters. Dragsters that went on to break the 200 mph barrier powered, of course, by the king of horsepower—the 392 ci Chrysler Hemi.

After winning the Division II National Hot Rod Association points championship in 1979, Mickey and his partner decided it was time to retire from drag racing. Retired from racing didn't mean retired from cars, though. So Mickey simply took his enthusiasm, combined with his considerable skills, and applied both to street rodding. When it came time to build the first car, there was no doubt as to the choice: The first car would be Mickey's favorite, a Deuce roadster powered by his favorite engine.

The red roadster didn't start out as a derelict from some farmer's field. Like an especially good cake, created without the help of a mix, Mickey's Deuce roadster was scratch-built.

Mickey and friends started with The Deuce Factory rails and went on to build a complete chassis. The rear end came from a '65 Ford, narrowed to fit. The axles are from Carroll Machine, while the aluminum third-member is from Mark Williams. The four-bar suspension is from that venerable Home-Built company and uses Spax coil-overs to keep the whole thing off the ground.

At the other end, the axle is a Super Bell with a 3 in. drop kept in place by a Home-Built four-bar and a buggy-style spring from Joe Smith Automotive. A Vega steering box points the way, connected by a Home-Built drag link to the right-side spindle assembly.

Other bits and pieces round out the chassis: The front brakes are Toyota calipers squeezing Vega rotors, while the rear drums are from a Mercury Marquis. The master cylinder is a Mustang unit and the proportioning valve is from a Dodge. The

What could be better than a Hemi-powered Deuce? Built along the lines of Bonneville roadsters and early drag cars, Mickey Cox built a Deuce roadster with the ultimate horsepower champ—a 354 ci Chrysler Hemi-head.

Gas tank of Mickey's roadster has been moved into the trunk. Unusual wheels were built by the owner using centers and rims intended for the roundy-round set.

unusual wheels are Mickey's own, welded up from Broad Wheel centers and rims, then slotted and painted to match the car.

The heart of Mickey's roadster is under the hood, a 354 ci Hemi. While it may not be an alcohol-powered dragster engine, it was assembled with the greatest of care and puts out some serious horsepower. Mickey started by sending the bare block out to Bob Amos at Music City Rod Shop for cleaning and a 0.060 in. overbore. Reassembly started with a stock Chrysler crank, shot-peened Chrysler rods and J&E 9.5:1 pistons, all balanced before assembly.

The cylinder heads on the '56 block are from the smaller, 331 ci Hemi. Another of the tricks Mickey learned during those years on the drag strip: the older Hemi heads actually flow more air than the latest (and presumably best) 392 ci heads. These heads have been ported and polished, and treated to a three-angle valve job at the hands of Gene Adams. The intake valves measure 2 1/16 in. (these are trimmed 426 ci Hemi valves) while the exhaust valves measure 1 7/8 in.

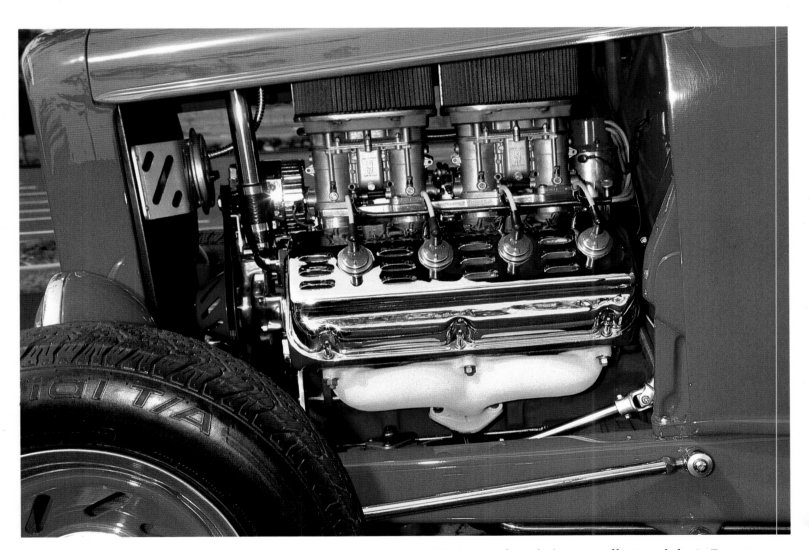

The engine is a 354 ci Chrysler Hemi with older 331 ci heads. The heads have been treated to a three-angle valve job and carry intake valves measuring 2 1/16 in. and exhausts measuring 1 7/8 in. The block was treated to a 0.060 in. overbore before installation of the J&E 9.5:1 pistons, Chrysler rods and Chrysler crank. The camshaft is from Engle while the carburetors are by Weber.

The first car would be Mickey's favorite, a Deuce roadster powered by his favorite engine

Operating those big valves is an Engle camshaft and lifters. The cam is relatively mild with .260 degree of duration and 0.440 in. of lift. Carburetion for this roadster is as unusual as everything else: four Weber carbs on a polished, Home-Built manifold.

The considerable power of the old Hemi is passed to the Ford rear end through a late-model Chrysler 727 Torqueflite. The Torqueflite has been rebuilt and beefed up by Tommy Shinholster, another of the drag racing fraternity.

The body Mickey chose for his Deuce is the well-known Wescott fiberglass roadster body. The lift-off top is Mickey's own while the louvered hood is from Rootlieb. The grille shell is from Wescott while the grille insert is from an original '32 Ford. An interesting detail, the windshield posts were cast from bronze using patterns created in Mickey's shop.

More interesting details can be found inside the roadster. The seats and door panels are covered in

This unique dashboard has the correct feel. Gauges are large, round and framed with gold-plated rings. Dash surface has been turned for the machined effect. Steering wheel might have come from an early Indy 500 racer.

Next page
Just the basics: Disc brake rotors have been ventilated to dissipate water. Dropped I-beam axle is held in place by buggy-style spring and owner-built four-bar suspension.

Gas tank is housed in forward section of the trunk. Fuel filler is reminiscent of early race cars.

gray, Connolly leather. The dashboard has been fabricated from a sheet of aluminum, turned to provide an interesting texture. The rings surrounding the mostly Stewart-Warner gauges are gold-plated and provide a nice accent. The Smiths tachometer is from an old record-holding inboard hydroplane. The steering wheel is from Bell, with a gray color to match the seats and a style that works in harmony with the rest of the interior.

Though it is different from so many of the Deuce roadsters seen at events, Mickey's red roadster is truly a classic Hiboy. Classic as in Bonneville or drag racing Hiboys. Hiboys stripped of all but the essentials with a whole lot of motor under the hood. The classic hot rod body mated to the classic hot rod engine. It just doesn't get any better than this.

A real roadster needs red paint, a 9 in. Ford rear end and Big Meats in the back.

Less is More

Knowing When to Say Whoa

When it comes to street rods, some people want it all. A car that's chopped, channeled, smoothed and painted in the latest neon scallops. Others, however, think it folly to tinker with a great design. These traditionalists feel that a design as eye-pleasing as Henry's '32 Ford should be left intact—that by leaving the design alone, less modification allows more of the original design to shine through.

When Paul Gilliam bought his Deuce in the late 1970s, the car was a complete runner. A nearly stock Ford with a Chevy small-block, but otherwise pretty much as it came off the line in 1932. The body was nearly perfect, with no rust, good steel fenders and no modifications.

Paul drove the Deuce for about a year before deciding it was time to fulfill his dream and build a really nice Deuce street rod. After the body came off the frame, Paul sent it to Ken Allen for fresh paint. Ken wanted to chop the top—he just couldn't see a Deuce Tudor without a lowered lid. Paul stuck to his guns. He knew what he wanted, a classic Deuce with classic lines.

Once the body was removed, an inspection turned up a bent frame. The car apparently had been hit once in the left rear. Though the body had been repaired, the frame had been kinked just a little and never straightened. After the frame was straightened, Paul and his friend Mickey Cox (whose Hemi roadster can be seen elsewhere in this book) used the frame to create a frame jig.

The jig had two purposes: First, it would allow them to cut the cross-members out of Paul's frame, manufacture new ones and correctly reassemble the frame. Second, the jig would allow them to build a new frame for Mickey's roadster using aftermarket rails and their own cross-members.

The frame they assembled for Paul's Tudor uses the stock rails, boxed at the front and rear. The front cross-member came from The Deuce Factory, while the center and rear cross-members were fabricated in their own shop. The center cross-member is actually an X-member, adding greatly to the frame's strength.

Paul Gilliam's Tudor makes a classy ride. Unchopped, the Tudor uses all the original styling cues, including stock bumpers, large headlights and even the cowl lights. Wire wheels work well with the traditional styling theme.

Signature of a '32 Ford. The stock grille shell and large headlights remind us why the Deuce became such a classic.

Once the frame was finished, Paul and Mickey fabricated their own four-bar suspensions for both the front and rear. At the front, the Ford commercial straight axle was first dropped 2½ in. and then chrome plated. The buggy-style spring is an original Ford unit with reversed eyes. The rear four-bar setup is a triangulated design with Aldan coil-overs locating a Mustang rear axle.

Before getting started on his street rod project, Paul bought a '79 Chevy wagon—the proverbial donor car. The first thing the Chevy donated was its

front disc brakes which Paul adapted to the '40 Ford spindles. Next came the 327 ci small-block and 400 Turbo transmission.

When it came to the engine for Paul's rod, he wanted a dependable powerplant, one he could just drive and drive without a worry. The 327 ci Chevy was disassembled, cleaned and sent out for a 0.030 in. overbore. Paul had the new pistons, Chevy rods and stock crank balanced before reassembly. The heads have been ported and polished, and carry 2.02 in. intakes and 1.80 in. exhaust valves. Operating those valves is a fairly mild camshaft from Competition Cams with 268 degrees of duration and 0.454 in. of lift.

Finally, Paul's almost new engine could be mated to the rebuilt transmission and installed in

Mild rather than wild—this small-block started life as a Chevrolet 327 ci engine. Rebuild included a 0.030 in. overbore, new pistons, and rods and crank from

Chevrolet. The heads have been treated to a thorough massage including new 2.02 in. intake and 1.80 in. exhaust valves.

Paul stuck to his guns. He knew what he wanted: a classic Deuce with classic lines

the frame. This left the frame ready to accept the ultra-straight body, with its fresh Ember Rust Fire Mist paint.

During the reassembly, Paul used accessories that work well with his Deuce's traditional lines: The large-diameter headlights sit on a chrome bar. The grille shell was left stock, right down to its Ford logo. The hood, too, is the one Henry built, as are the small cowl lights, not often seen on the street rods these days.

The interior of Paul's Deuce is a combination of old and new. The dashboard has been left mostly intact, with its small central insert. The insert itself is Paul's own, fabricated from aluminum, housing the speedometer, fuel and temperature gauges. At either end of the dashboard small vents for the air conditioner indicate that no, this isn't really 1932. Above the front seat is another of those modern conveniences, the sliding sunroof. Covering the seats and door panels is a rich brown velour, stitched up by Lester Rice from Harriman, Tennessee.

Paul's Deuce has been on the road for seven years now. During those years it has required nothing more than standard maintenance. Paul says, "I built this one to drive. We put on over 9,000 miles a year—so far without any trouble."

Interior has been stitched up using a brown velour often used in new GM cars. The dashboard and insert are near- stock, though Henry never built one with air-conditioning outlets.

The rear of the body follows themes started at the front: stock gas tank, bumper and taillights. Subtle pinstriping is similar to what the car might have carried in 1932.

Front axle is a Ford commercial I-beam, dropped 2½ in. Suspension is a home-built four-bar using a buggy-style spring with reversed eyes. Front brakes are discs of GM origin.

Seven years after it was built, Paul's Tudor still looks good. Alongside a more radical street rod, the Tudor looks somehow more composed. Like a truly beautiful woman, Paul's Deuce doesn't need flames or jewelry to look good. When the latest techno-rod goes in for a refit because what's "in" has changed, Paul's classic Tudor will still look great. Three fads from now, Paul will still be driving the Tudor—a rolling testament to classic styling and good taste.

A "Spiritual" Hot Rod

A Deuce That Stirs the Soul

Some hot rodders get an early start—like Doug Wamsher, who got his first car at age 12 when Mom and Dad gave it to him. The car was a '48 Plymouth, but what Doug remembers best was a ride he and Dad took in a neighbor's Ford coupe at about the same time. The coupe was a Deuce powered by a Flathead with three 97s. Doug remembers that the car was pretty rough, with no interior and wires hanging down below the dash—but it was the most thrilling ride he'd ever had. Doug had been introduced to hot rodding, and the introduction left a deep impression.

That '48 Plymouth was only the first in a long series of cars. There have been a collection of early Fords, a Corvette and a Trans Am Pontiac built for the racetrack. Yet, somehow none of these cars really fit the bill. While all were nice and some were fast, none of them captured that spirit—the true spirit of a hot rod—like the old Ford coupe with the Flathead.

Doug's quest finally came to an end early in 1989. An ad in a magazine described a '32 Ford with a blown small-block. After looking the coupe over, Doug realized that the price was right and that with a little work it just might turn into the car he'd always been wanting.

Like his father before him, Doug believes the car hobby should be a family affair. Thus, Doug's two sons, Brandon and Ryan, pitched in to help transform the coupe from an "almost right" to a "perfect" hot rod.

The car they brought home was a runner. A fiberglass, three-window Deuce coupe body set on boxed frame rails with four-bar suspension at both ends. The new ride might best be described as a little rough. A close inspection revealed a solid engine and good supercharger, though the carburetors needed some help. The chassis and suspension proved to be in good condition and could be left intact.

A large part of the work necessary on the coupe involved the three-window body. First, Doug had two stainless-steel gas tanks fabricated by Bill's Custom Shop of Ottawa Lake, Michigan, and mounted them under the car. Once the new tanks were installed, Doug took off the old tank and delivered the coupe to Wilkinson's Body shop of Sylvania, Ohio.

Tom Wilkinson formed a nice rolled pan where the tank used to be and frenched-in the '39 Ford taillights. Other bodywork included refitting both doors and finishing the job of filling the roof. When all the adjusting and massaging of the body panels was finished, Tom sprayed the coupe bright red.

Making the car run as good as it looked required rebuilding and adjusting both Holley carbs—the work was done by Mark Moses. The Dyers

From this angle the three-window coupe seems to be all engine and tires. The very red coupe carries a serious blown small-block.

Two days spent cruising the grounds, going out for pizza—just the guys you understand—does wonders for a father-son relationship

Two Holley carbs feed the GMC-Dyers blower. Engine is a 350 small-block using low-compression pistons and Chevrolet rods and crank. Considerable horsepower is passed to a GM Turbo 350 transmission.

supercharger was deemed to be in good condition and, other than a thorough tune-up, the engine was ready to run. Like the motor, the Turbo 350 automatic transmission worked without a flaw and was simply left alone.

But Doug wanted more than just a fast '32 coupe. His goal was "a good old-fashioned hot rod." Doug wanted a car that "looks like it's going 100 miles per hour when it's sitting still." Big and little tires, without fenders, are a big part of that look. Doug's coupe rides on enormous 33x19.5x15 in.

The rear mirrors' front view. This is where all that horsepower is translated into motion. Gas tank has been moved to make room for the wheelie bars and the rear pan.

61

Just the basics: A dropped axle, disc brakes, tube shocks and a four-bar suspension.

Maybe the soul of that old coupe somehow has been transplanted to Doug's new Deuce

Mickey Thompson tires in back and skinny 165x15 Kelly metrics in front. Wheelie bars reinforce the go-fast image, as does the chrome scoop mounted over the carburetors.

When it was all finished Doug, Brandon and Ryan took the new Deuce coupe to the Goodguys Indy Happening, the three of them with their two cars (Brandon and Ryan in their Model A) for a weekend of street rodding. Two days spent cruising the grounds, going out for pizza—just the guys, you understand—does wonders for a father-son relationship.

For Doug, the best part of the trip to Indy was driving his new coupe. It may not have a Flathead and it may be a little too "nice," but it does truly and finally capture the spirit of hot rodding—as though maybe the soul of that old coupe somehow has been transplanted to Doug's new Deuce.

An unusual view. Radiator catch-tank has been chromed, along with almost everything else. Suspension is a four-bar, front brakes are discs.

Long, Tall Sally

A Rock'n'Roll Deuce Pickup

Music and cars. The two run together, intertwined in our culture and in the life of Bob Massey. When asked why be built a Deuce pickup and why there are two Deuces in his garage, Bob explains: "Well, I used to play in a small rock 'n' roll band, and one of the songs that we played—and one of my favorites—was 'Little Deuce Coupe.' I decided then, that if I ever had a hot rod it was going to be a Deuce."

Bob's dream came true in 1982 when he bought a three-window coupe. Life was good; his dream car sat gleaming in the garage. Everything was fine until 1985 when Bob attended the Street Rod Nationals in St. Paul, Minnesota.

Among all the other street rods Bob spied was this particular black, '32 Ford truck. It was a Deuce and it had these great proportions. Both the top and the bed were stock, making the truck look long and

tall compared to most of the other early pickups at the event.

That image of the black Deuce with the long bed and the unchopped top stayed with Bob and soon he decided that his next vehicle would have to be another Deuce, a Deuce truck.

The end result of that dream, Bob's yellow Deuce truck, started life in North Dakota, land of howling wind and minimal body rust. During the summer of 1985 Bob was cleaning the garage when he spied a recent issue of *Hemmings Motor News* sitting on the bench. Paging through to the middle of the Ford listings—always more fun than cleaning the garage—Bob found a listing for a 1932 Ford pickup truck.

One lengthy phone call later, Bob had agreed to buy the rust-free truck for $775. The trip from Joplin, Missouri, to Fargo, North Dakota, would make a story in itself. The trip there included time out for a bad fuel pump, and of course the truck itself wasn't quite as nice as Bob had been led to believe—but it wasn't bad enough to make Bob leave it there, either. The trip home included the blizzard of the century—at least it looked that way to Bob as he drove through it.

Yet, as Bob started the complete disassembly in his home garage, all the toil and trouble seemed to be worth it. The body was nearly rust free and it was nearly all there. The fenders were rough, the roof had a number of dents and a few of the small parts were missing, but all in all it wasn't too bad.

The frame hadn't fared well during all those years on the prairie, however, so Bob had Curt Cunningham of Carriage Works assemble a new frame based on The Deuce Factory rails. At the front Curt used a Pete and Jake's four-bar suspension, tied

The unchopped top and stock-length bed give this Deuce pickup a look that is seldom seen these days. Tailgate with the Ford script is actually from a '35 pickup.

Clean and simple. The white upholstery was stitched up by Bob Sipes. Dash is close to Henry Ford's version, with three gauges in the small aluminum panel.

Previous page
Large-diameter commercial lights work in harmony with the stock body proportions. Smooth hood sides were built by Bob while the hood is by Rootlieb. Chrome dropped axle is from Super Bell as are the spindles and rotors. Front suspension is a four-bar from Pete and Jake's.

Bob's yellow Deuce truck, started life in North Dakota, land of howling wind and minimal body rust

to a Super Bell axle with a 4 in. drop, and a Posies leaf spring. The front spindles and rotors are from Super Bell while the calipers are from a Volkswagen. The steering chores are handled by Vega steering gear mounted to the left frame rail and tied to the right spindle assembly in cross-steer fashion.

At the rear, the Ford 9 in. rear end came out of a '60 T-Bird, narrowed to fit the Deuce frame. Spax coil-overs and a four-bar linkage from Pete and Jake's keep everything off the ground and pointing straight down the road.

While Curt and the boys were busy building the frame, Bob was busy building and detailing the engine. Originally a Chevy 327, Bob started the rebuild with a 0.030 in. overbore and a complete balance job before beginning the assembly. The pistons Bob installed are from TRW, connected to Chevy rods and a steel crank. The Chevrolet heads are double-hump models treated to a three-angle valve job before installation. Operating those valves is a stock Chevrolet camshaft, while the carb is a Carter four-barrel breathing through a polished manifold.

Before installing the engine in the new frame, Bob ground all the lumps off the block and painted it to match the body. Then he polished the 350 Turbo tranny's entire case before bolting it to the engine.

As the chassis neared completion Bob made plans to finish the body. Like the truck he had seen in St. Paul, this Deuce truck would keep a stock top and stock bed length. Bob was willing to do some of the bodywork himself, but for the tough jobs he relied on the metal working skills of Curt Cunningham.

Because the truck had little rust, Bob and Curt had only to straighten it, make a few alterations to Henry's original plan and get some paint on it. Curt did most of bodywork on the cab, filling in the cowl vent and straightening the doors. Curt doesn't like body filler, so after welding the patch into the cowl vent, he showed his metal working skills by finishing the repair without one ounce of Bondo.

The roof with its many small dents and all the smaller details became Bob's responsibility.

Learning as he went, Bob took the thirty-five dents out of the roof and then built his own aluminum firewall. The more he looked at the box, the less he liked what he saw. Finally he drove to Mack Products Company in Moberly, Missouri, and bought a new box and a tailgate from a '35 Ford pickup. Most people don't notice the difference, but the later tailgate has the classic Ford script across the surface—a feature lacking on the '32 tailgate.

At the other end of the truck, Bob used a Wescott smooth grille shell, The Deuce Factory dropped headlight bar and two, large-diameter commercial headlights to keep the traditional theme. The hood sides are more of Bob's own handiwork, formed from sheet steel, while the hood top is from Rootlieb.

Like the truck he had seen in St. Paul, this Deuce truck would keep a stock top and stock bed length

The paint on this Deuce is called Chrome Yellow, a stock Ford truck color (what else?) from 1979. As the cab and body sections were finished, Bob painted each piece in his small shop at home. The original fenders were just too far gone, so glass fenders were used at all four corners. Finally, after nearly a full year of preparation, Bob could bolt all the pieces into a complete, finished '32 Ford truck.

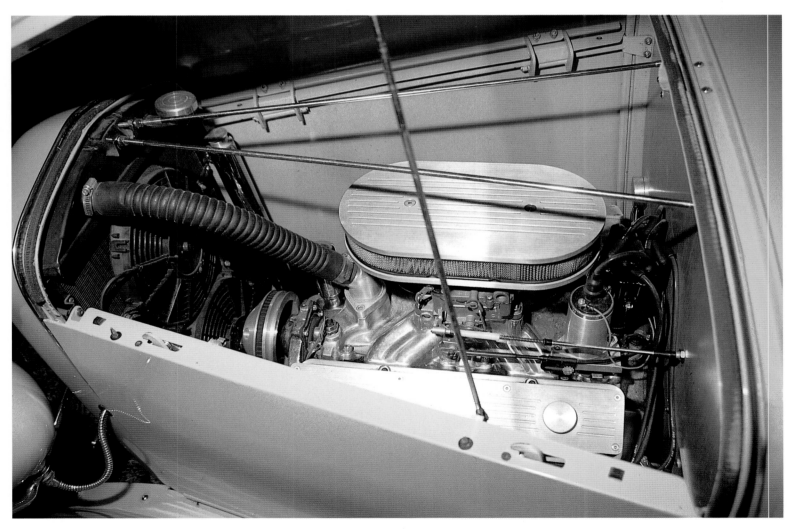

The small-block is a 327 by Chevrolet, completely rebuilt by the owner. Internals include TRW pistons, stock rods and crank. A Carter four-barrel carb feeds fuel through the ported and polished heads, past valves operated by a stock Chevy cam.

The paint on Bob Massey's truck is a Ford hue known as
Chrome Yellow. Chrome or not, the paint picks up a nice
glow from the late-afternoon sun.

Though the body is steel, the rear fenders are fiberglass.
Like the front, the rear lights work well with the stock
body proportions and traditional theme.

Putting the Hot Back in Hot Rod

Good Time Slips and Air Conditioning Too

The only thing missing was the interior, and there was a catch. The earliest Bob could get the truck up to Bob Sipes for the interior was Monday morning. The problem was the approaching Street Rod Nats the following weekend. Bob wanted to leave on Tuesday night. Impossible? Not when one of Sipes' other appointments didn't show up on Monday morning and the entire crew could work together sewing up the white vinyl interior for the yellow truck. Yes, Bob picked up his truck Tuesday afternoon and left for the Nats later that night.

That maiden voyage was made in 1987, 700 miles on an untested truck. Everything went just fine, however, and Bob has driven his truck to every Nationals since. He reports that the old car goes down the road just fine, that even with the relatively mild small-block she seems truly built for speed.

During some of those highway trips Bob recalls another of his favorite songs from his rock 'n roll days, an old Elvis song titled, "Long, Tall Sally." One stanza talks about Long, Tall Sally, built sweet, with everything uncle John needs. The next stanza goes on to explain that Long, Tall Salley was built for speed. Yes, she's got everything that uncle Bob needs.

When David and Carol Tallant started planning their new car, a '32 Ford three-window coupe, they didn't budget for lots of the latest, trick billet aluminum bits and pieces. This Deuce would include no killer stereos, no small-block Chevy engines and no eurotech paint schemes.

Instead, David and Carol planned a coupe that would be, quite simply, a good old-fashioned hot rod. Instead of billet bits and pieces from a catalog, David prefers to fabricate his own. In place of the standard small-block, David and Carol chose a giant killer: a big-block Chevy motor with a GMC huffer mounted on top. These two street rodders wanted a rod that was hot, but not too wild to use as a daily driver.

The coupe that David purchased was far from nice. An old drag race car, the three-window came with the trunk and doors welded shut, no interior, no inner doors and almost no dashboard. The original Deuce rails were beat-up and bent.

While some builders would have discarded the original frame and started over with aftermarket parts, David took a different approach. He explains: "I get a tremendous amount of satisfaction from building a car. Part of that satisfaction comes from repairing all the old worn-out pieces and fabricating the things that are missing."

David repaired the old Deuce rails and fabricated new cross-members. The design goal was a frame that would accommodate some serious, pro-

Built to run. David and Carol Tallant built a Deuce they would never have to apologize for. This one provides time slips in the 12s and an air-conditioned ride to and from the strip.

> *"A blower motor will make its own power. That blower will push the fuel and air through the engine; you've just got to let it work and give it lots of air on top and a nice open exhaust at the other end."*

street rear rubber and the attendant suspension. Like so much of the car, the rear suspension is hand-built: a four-bar of David's design using Spax coil-over shocks.

Some people say you can't use the popular Mustang II front suspension under a Deuce due to insufficient room under the fenders for the spring towers. David agrees that room under the fenders is tight, but has his own solution to the problem: "We moved the upper spring mount down and out to clear the fenders. Of course that changes the geometry, so we shorten the upper control arm and build extensions for the ends of the rack and pinion. We experimented until we could move the suspension through its complete range (with no springs or shocks of course) and experience no change in the toe-in."

The hottest part of David and Carol's rod is definitely the big-block Chevy with all its glorious chrome and polish. The engine started out as a 454 Chevrolet block bored 0.030 in. over for a total displacement of 462 ci. The forged pistons are from TRW and carry an 8.25:1 compression ratio. Those big slugs are connected to stock Chevy connecting rods and a Chevrolet steel crankshaft.

David used a relatively mild cam from Competition Cams with 280 degrees of duration and 0.527 in. of lift to operate the stock valvetrain. He explains why there are no trick valve jobs or porting: "A blower motor will make its own power. That blower will push the fuel and air through the engine; you've just got to let it work and give it lots of air on top and a nice open exhaust at the other end."

Back to its roots. The car was an old refugee from the drag strip when David bought it. Originally a 454, this big-block has been bored 0.030 in. over, and carries TRW 8.25:1 pistons. Rods and crank are stock Chevrolet items. Supercharger is a GMC 6-71 from Dyers. Carburetion is by twin Carter four barrels. Assembled with lots of TLC, the combination works out to around 550 hp.

"It turns 12.50s at the strip with street tires and mufflers—not too bad for a 3,250 lb. car. Then we drive it home with the air conditioning on."

Two Carter 625 cfm AFB carbs provide the air on top. Getting the exhaust out is accomplished with a set of chrome exhaust manifolds, large-diameter exhaust pipes and two Supertrapp mufflers. The unusual valve covers with ribs to match the GMC blower are more of David's handiwork.

Estimates put the big-block in the 550 hp range, enough horsepower to twist the planetaries out of an

Comin' at ya. Independent front suspension is a modified Mustang II. Three electric fans and two radiators help to cool the supercharged big-block equipped with air conditioning. The frame has been modified to accept larger-than-life rear rubber. Suspension is a four-bar built by the car's owner. Indy Raceway Park officials wouldn't let the coupe run during the Goodguys event due to some "insurance" problems with blown cars.

ordinary automatic transmission. The solution was a 400 Series Turbo Hydro-matic with a manual valve body and a 2000 rpm stall converter. The short driveshaft was made up in David's shop and connects to a Mopar 8¾ in. rear end with a narrowed housing using Mark Williams axles.

Once the frame and engine were complete, David could turn his attention to the old coupe body. Though there wasn't any rust, that doesn't mean the restoration was an easy task. First, the doors and trunk had to be cut free of the body where they were welded shut. Next, the door edges and inner panels had to be fabricated from scratch. The dashboard too had been badly cut up and had to be re-created.

As the cutting and repairing continued, it became apparent that the top—the one part of the car that David thought was already finished—had been chopped incorrectly. In order to make everything else fit right, the top had to be recut and correctly welded back together.

As the body started to come together there were all the small details to take care of: Things like the homemade, cable-operated power windows, the new solenoid-actuated Pinto door latches, and a gauge cluster to mount in the center of the new dashboard.

The final paint color is a special red that David had mixed especially for the car. A bright red without any orange—a most appropriate color for a hot, hot rod.

Nearly one year after starting, the Deuce coupe was almost finished. There was only one thing left, one job that even David would have to farm out to another craftsman—the upholstery. The coupe's tan threads were stitched up by North Kansas City Auto Trim with special "Big-Block" door panels fabricated by Mick's Upholstery. Ventilation is provided by a functional cowl vent and air conditioning.

The air conditioning created a potential overheating problem, a problem solved in an unusual fashion. David already had the largest Walker radiator that would fit the Deuce grille shell. The folks at Walker advised against air conditioner use with the blower motor. Well, David went ahead and mounted the condenser in front of the radiator anyway, and then used three electric fans to move air across the fins. And because even that probably wouldn't be enough on a really broiling summer day, a *second* radiator was mounted under the car. This second set of tubes started life as a GM air conditioner evaporator plumbed into the cooling

David Tallant leans on the coupe he built. When asked how he learned all the various skills needed to build a car such as this, David replies: "When I was about 15 years old I had this mini bike and I asked this painter how much it would cost to do a metal-flake paint job. The guy said $150. Well, I didn't have that kind of money so I borrowed a paint gun and bought some paint and one thing just kind of led to another . . . ."

system the same way a heater core would be—with its own, thermostatically controlled electric fan.

When it was all over, there was the inevitable question: Did they succeed? On all counts the answer would have to be a resounding yes. The coupe is definitely a hot rod, with both the right look and good time slips. David sums it all up when he says: "This car makes it to runs under its own power. It turns 12.50s at the strip with street tires and mufflers—not too bad for a 3,250 pound car. Then we drive it home with the air conditioning on."

A Wide-Open Deuce

Built to Cruise

he answers: "I'd already owned three Deuce Hiboys and needed something new." The phaeton started out as a Wescott fiberglass body that Barry found at a local swap meet. Another street rodder's unfinished project, Barry took the glass body home and made plans to build one a little different from most.

Though Barry lists his occupation as machinist, he is a man of many talents. At the time he bought the phaeton body, Barry had just finished building a series of Deuce frames. One more frame was in order and like the others, Barry built it with The Deuce Factory rails and custom cross-members. To get the right stance, he chose a Super Bell tube axle with a 4 in. drop. The four-bar suspension was built in his home shop and uses a single, buggy-style spring. Everything seems normal enough until you look at the shocks. They aren't the tube-style shocks normally seen on street rods. They are lever-action shocks, closer to what Henry used on the original Deuce. Originally built for an MG, Barry likes the lever shocks for their ride quality and the fact that the ride can be made softer or stiffer just by changing the fluid.

The rear suspension, too, is a four-bar of home manufacture and utilizes a panhard rod to absorb the side loads. The coil-overs are from Aldan and feature adjustable damping rates. Barry's choice for a rear axle is the hard-to-find assembly from a Lincoln Versailles. The Lincoln rear axle combines the advantages of factory disc brakes with the bulletproof Ford 9 in. center section, all in a relatively narrow package. The front brakes are discs too, with rotors and calipers from a late-model Mustang adapted to the '48 Ford spindles.

For a man who likes both '32 Fords and open cars, a Deuce phaeton would be the perfect street rod. Barry Larson of Anoka, Minnesota, is just such a man. When asked why he built the Deuce phaeton,

A modern Deuce phaeton, Barry Larson's open car is based on a Wescott glass body. Hood sides with their unusual vents were crafted by the owner. Unusual wheels are from MSW; metric hole spacing was modified to match a Ford pattern.

80

No detail is too small. The rear brakelights on the Phaeton are both traditional and modern.

As Barry contemplated the finished car, he thought it should be modern and clean. No nostalgia rod, his phaeton would be thoroughly modern. Barry's first task was eliminating the external hinges. The new hidden hinges were fabricated in his home shop. Barry remembers: "It took me almost one week of evenings, per door, to mount the hinges and then adjust everything so the door gap turned out even."

Barry knew that achieving the correct look for the phaeton would mean getting the right shape for the top. A strong believer in that old adage, If you want something done right . . . , Barry set about building a new top mechanism. At the front there's a set of chopped stainless windshield posts and a matching windshield. From the windshield back, everything was built by hand. Barry made the folding framework from flat stock and asked his wife Joan for help in shaping and laminating the birch top bows. The lines of the new top—covered

Small-block V-8 is a truck engine purchased new from Chevrolet. Intake manifold is from Edelbrock while the carburetor is a 650 Holley. Horsepower is more than adequate and available relatively low in the rpm range.

with Cadillac convertible top material—are very nice, obviously lower but also rounder than the original.

The phaeton's front sheet metal is kind of a collaboration between Henry Ford and Barry: the grille shell is Henry's, filled and smoothed, with a hand-built insert by Barry. The hood is also by Barry, with custom hood sides featuring vents of his own design.

The powerplant for this open Deuce is a four-bolt 350 truck engine ordered new from Chevrolet. Breathing through a 650 Holley on an Edelbrock intake manifold, the engine creates plenty of power to pull the 2,600 lb. street rod. Behind the 350 engine is an unusual transmission—a Muncie four-speed!

As the phaeton started to come together it was time to think about the bodywork and final paint.

"It took six complete hides to get the whole thing covered—I asked Keith if maybe these were small cows?"

Barry did most of the bodywork himself, with help from Jim Brown and Bobby Gage. After all the bodywork and all the block-sanding was completed, the Deuce was taken to Superior Auto Body in Ramsey, Minnesota, where Dave Robidue applied the Porsche India Red paint and clear coat.

The final job, the interior, was done by Keith Nybo from New Brighton, Minnesota. The material is leather, and as Barry remembers: "The leather wasn't cheap. It took six complete hides to get the

Door panels and seats are covered in leather. Unique dash with neat cluster of round gauges was built by the owner.

Note the clutch pedal and shift knob—this street rod relies on the owner for gear changes.

84

Front suspension is a four-bar with a buggy-style spring and lever shocks. Axle is from Super Bell, dropped 4 in.

Steering is handled by a Vega gear connected in cross-steer fashion to the right side.

whole thing covered—I asked Keith if maybe these were small cows?" The interior is done in beige and the door panels repeat the vent design used on the hood. Keith also covered Barry's hand-built top mechanism. Both the dashboard and gauge panel were fabricated from aluminum, with accent pieces fashioned on Barry's Bridgeport mill.

The project was finished early in 1988, just in time for the annual Gopher State Timing Association show in St. Paul, Minnesota. Some people might think that an open car like the phaeton isn't real practical—that after a few shows it might

end up as a garage queen. Both Barry and his wife Joan would argue with that. The phaeton gets used—a lot. Like the roadsters that went before it, this open Deuce will rack up lots of miles. Barry and Joan are the kind of people who think nothing of taking an open car out of state, or all the way to the West Coast.

Barry Larson really likes open Deuces—in fact, he likes them best when they're going down the road and all you can hear is the sound of the pipes and the wind in your ears.

85

Rear end is from a Lincoln Versailles, a Ford 9 in. with disc brakes to boot. Rear suspension is a four-bar with coil-overs and a panhard rod.

Grille insert is built by Barry from bar stock, then painted black. Door hinges have disappeared in favor of hidden hinges and the modern look.

Black Glass

Ultra-Smooth and Black to Boot

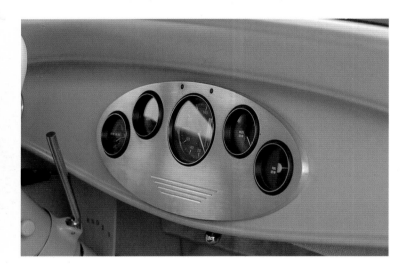

People with black street rods have to understand that although their cars may look great, they don't usually end up as feature material. Why? Because they're just too hard to photograph. If the photographer isn't careful, the beautiful black car ends up looking like an ordinary, black blob. Yet, some of those black beauties are so well done, with the paint as smooth as a fresh sheet of glass, they just beg for the photographer's extra attention.

The black five-window coupe of Lon Lewis is one such car. Recently rebuilt, the black coupe is very black and very straight. It takes guts to put such shiny black paint on a car that's almost sixty years old.

There is no brightwork here. No bumpers. No chrome headlight rings. No chrome taillight bezels. Just those great original Deuce lines. The headlights stand on small, black pedestals. The taillights are integrated into the spreader bar. The door and trunk handles have disappeared, replaced by electronic

solenoids. The effect is clean and modern—exactly what Lon had in mind when he started the rebuild in 1987.

Lon got involved with street rods some fifteen years ago when a friend asked for help building a Model A. By the time they finished the Model A, Lon knew he wanted a car of his own. He liked the looks of his friend's Model A and thought he might build one for himself—until he got a good look at a Deuce coupe. The Deuce had lines that seemed to flow better, were somehow cleaner than those of the Model A. Needless to say, the street rod Lon purchased in 1976 wasn't a Model A but a Deuce, a five-window Deuce coupe.

The coupe made a great street rod. In eleven years Lon put more than 60,000 miles on the clock. During those years the car evolved, going through two paint changes and gaining a few amenities like air conditioning. In 1987, Lon decided it was time to give up evolution and prepare for the revolution. The goal of Lon's revolution was a more modern car, both in performance and appearance.

The performance part of the equation started in Lon's home shop with a complete disassembly. He chose to keep the Deuce frame, reinforcing it with new cross-members. At the rear, the Corvette independent rear end and suspension were left intact. At the front, however, the straight axle was discarded in favor of independent suspension borrowed from a Jaguar E-Type. The Jaguar spindle

An American tradition: A pair of Deuces at the drive-in. The neon signs reflected in the satin black paint. Top has been chopped and the roof filled, though the cowl vent remains. This Deuce has just enough rake to create the right look. Red roadster belongs to Bob John.

Pages 90-91
Low angle shows off the Corvette rear suspension. Note the clouds reflected in the deep pools of black paint. This is a lovely, modern Deuce coupe. Door handles and hinges are hidden for the smooth and sanitary look. Metal work is flawless and contains many unusual details—note the missing "bead" at the edge of the cowl and grille shell.

There is no brightwork here. No bumpers. No chrome headlight rings. No chrome taillight bezels. Just those great original Deuce lines

assemblies are tied to a Chrysler K car rack and pinion. Next, the old 283 was removed in favor of a brand-new 350—one of Chevrolet's four-bolt Target Master engines. The motor is basically stock, equipped with chrome pulleys, polished aluminum valve covers and a Holley carburetor.

The appearance part of Lon's program started at A&R Auto in West Babylon, New York. The boys at A&R took about 3 in. out of the coupe's top, giving it the look needed by a modern, wind cheating kind of machine. They also filled the roof and eliminated the small bead at the front edge of the cowl.

Following the work of A&R, the coupe went to the small shop of Steve Pronechen for the finish work and paint. Steve had the coupe for more than a year. During that time he blocked out the body and spent considerable time making sure everything fit just right. Only after each body panel was perfect and each door seam uniform did Steve apply the Dupont Cronar black paint.

Previous page
Front seats started life in a Dodge Colt; steering column is from a Cadillac. Leather and fabric interior was stitched up by Masters Upholstery. Dash insert is from Carriage Works, gauges are S-W.

Throw out the old Chevy 283 and put a brand new Chevrolet small-block 350 truck engine in its place—a sure recipe for street power. This is a four-bolt Target Master with chromed pulleys, polished aluminum valve covers and a Holley carb on top.

The effect is clean and modern— exactly what Lon had in mind when he started the rebuild in 1987

Lon thought the inside of his pride and joy should be upgraded as well. Masters Upholstery from Newton, New Jersey, transformed Lon's ideas into a clean and elegant interior. The seats are from a Dodge Colt, covered in leather; the matching carpets are done in wool. The aluminum dash insert is from Carriage Works and holds Stewart-Warner Stage III gauges. The steering wheel is also leather covered and mounts to a Cadillac tilt and telescopic steering column.

Put it all together and what have you got? A Deuce for the nineties. A Deuce immaculate enough to make at least one photographer put aside his hang-ups about black cars.

Gas tank resides in the usual spot. Spreader bar is painted body color and contains the brake and taillights.

Headlights float on pedestals—hood sides are smooooth.

A Pair of Deuces

Better than a Full House Any Day

Possessing a certain continental elegance, the Ford Victoria was one of Edsel's favorite bodystyles. The two cars seen here have kept their elegance and composure—with important updates for the 1990s.

The two cars share more than just a bodystyle. Both represent the best of high-tech street rods. Both show bright red body panels minus extraneous bits like door hinges and handles. And both ride on sophisticated chassis with fully independent suspensions and all-wheel disc brakes.

Yet, each car offers its own version of high tech. Each offers a new twist on the "smooth" theme and each looks very different in profile. Each of these Ford Vickys reflects the individual tastes of the owners and builders.

Fred Sells the Vicky to Gus

The first of our two Victorias started as the project of Fred Warren. Fred had found the steel Ford body in the Deep South, bought it and took it to the Coming Attractions shop in Paducah, Kentucky. Fred wanted an ultra-clean Vicky. A high-tech street rod with all the latest hardware and the best equipment.

At the same time that Fred was starting on his Victoria another street rodder, Gus Ross, was looking for a new project. Gus explains: "My '34 three-window was finished, I was bored and looking for something to do with my hands." Gus was calling around, looking for a body or chassis that would be the start of a new project. When Gus called Coming Attractions to see how much it might be to build a Deuce chassis, he heard about Fred Warren's nice steel Vicky.

At that time the crew at Coming Attractions had finished Fred's chassis and started on the body. The chassis they built was based on some of the best equipment available to street rodders. At the front they used Strange Engineering hubs and tubular A-frames—all polished of course. The brake rotors too came from Strange, while the calipers are polished units from JFZ. The rear suspension uses a Corvette center section with inboard JFZ brakes and tapered axle shafts. Polished Aldan coil-overs are used at all four corners.

Despite the finished chassis and the chopped top, Fred felt that the project had lost momentum and maybe it was time to sell the unfinished Vicky. To make a long story short, Fred and Gus got together on the phone and soon the car changed hands.

Following the purchase of his new baby, Gus contracted with Coming Attractions to finish the bodywork on the car. Though the top had already

Two Vickys, smooth, red and clean—the same only different. Gus' car, right, is powered by a four-bolt 350 featuring 8.5:1 pistons connected to Chevy rods and crank. The heads carry 2.02 in. intake valves fed through Weber carbs mounted to a polished cross-ram intake manifold.

In the foreground is Fred Warren's Boyd Coddington-built car; farther back is Gus Ross' car with metal work by Coming Attractions. Both have chopped tops, yet the final effect is very different.

been cut 3 in., there was an enormous amount of work left to do. Larry Calhoun and the crew at Coming Attractions went ahead and finished cutting the doors, filling the roof and designing a new three-piece hood for the car.

The hood for Gus' car would be a little different than most Deuces because the wheelbase had been stretched 3 in. when the chassis was built. Fred explains: "The idea was a longer car with more length at the front to avoid that somewhat stubby

look the Victorias sometimes get—and of course it helps to provide a little more room under the hood."

Nearly one year after buying the car, Gus brought his unfinished Vicky home to the barn near his house. It was in the fall and he and his friend Corky Under set a work schedule of three hours per night, six nights per week. According to Gus: "The schedule was a good compromise—we got a lot done but we never got burned-out. Besides, it beat the hell out of sitting in front of the TV every night."

Understated and elegant, the interior of Gus' car is the work of Bob Snively High Tech Interiors. Bucket seats are GM units. *Dashboard is digital; 60 watt stereo resides in overhead console.*

Corky had the responsibility for things like the wiring and much of the remaining mechanical work. Meanwhile, Gus obtained a rebuilt small-block from Southern Ohio Engine Rebuilders in Middleton, Ohio. A single Holley just wouldn't do so Gus installed four Inglese-Weber sidedraft carburetors on a polished cross-ram intake manifold. To complement the polished manifold, Gus bolted on a set of polished pulleys from Street and Performance, and a pair of Corvette ribbed valve covers. Behind the shiny small-block Gus bolted in an equally shiny, rebuilt Turbo 350 automatic transmission.

Gus and Corky stayed with their schedule, plugging away throughout the winter. The only time they took a night off was when the temperature went below zero as it does in western Ohio and it got too cold to work in the unheated barn. As the

weather began to warm up, it was time to think about the paint job and interior for the new ride.

The Monstral Red finish paint was applied by John Childers at the C&W Body Shop in Brookville, Ohio. Next, the bright red beauty was taken to Bob Snively's High Tech Interiors in Richmond, Indiana. When the car came to Bob, the digital dash and Chevrolet steering column had already been installed by Coming Attractions. Bob designed and installed the gray interior. The bucket seats and door panels are covered in the same gray contract fabric. The 60 watt stereo is housed overhead and powers two sets of speakers with a separate 15 in. woofer.

Since finishing the car, Gus has taken a series of honors, including Ridler finalist at the Detroit Autorama show, Boyd's Pro Pick at the Goodguys

Indy event and Top 25 at Pigeon Forge. The awards help to justify all the work and the considerable outlay of cash. A man doesn't often get to own one of the best—as judged by his peers. For Gus Ross, this is one of those times.

Fred Needs a Vicky Afterall

During the year that Gus' Vicky was under construction, Fred Warren, the car's original owner, stopped by a few times to check on the progress. As the car neared completion, Fred could see that the project he started was going to be a nice car. During the summer of 1989 Fred went to the Nationals in St. Paul, Minnesota, and saw another ultra-clean Deuce Vicky built by none other than Boyd Coddington.

Boyd's car was eventually sold to a gentleman in Springfield, Missouri. Fred contacted the new car's owner—admiring his recently acquired street rod. As it turned out, Fred had an extra car—a nice Deuce roadster. After a couple of conversations, Fred was able to convince the Vicky's owner that a swap was in his best interests—that what he really needed was an open car. Fred of course came home with the new Vicky.

Boyd Coddington has quite a reputation, and he certainly lived up to that reputation when he built Fred's Vicky. The car is similar, yet different from the car Fred originally started out to build. It's close enough, though, that this could be the car Fred originally had in mind.

A high-tech street rod needs a high-tech chassis. Boyd, one of the originators of high tech, put his

A perfect blend of form and function. This beautiful front suspension uses Strange Engineering hubs and rotors connected to tubular, polished A-arms. Brake calipers are from JFZ, steering rack is from a Fiat.

The machinery isn't just functional or high tech, it's absolutely gorgeous

own chassis and suspension under the Vicky. The suspension is independent at both ends. The polished front A-frames and spindle assemblies are also Boyd's, and the calipers and rotors are from JFZ. The rear suspension starts with a Corvette center section coupled to Boyd's own polished hubs and locating links. The inboard disc brakes are by JFZ. The machinery isn't just functional or high tech, it's absolutely gorgeous.

The body, too, holds a few unique tricks. People who look closely at the car can see that the profile

has changed, but they aren't sure how. While the other Vicky sports a top dropped a full 3 in., this West Coast wonder has been chopped less than 2 in. In fact, the top has been cut more in the front than the back for a subtle taper.

The grille shell was chopped too and a new, Dan Fink hood was formed to run from the lowered grille shell to the cowl. The cut grille shell means the hood line also runs at a taper and makes the nose of the car look noticeably smaller. At the other end, the gas tank has been moved and a neat pan formed between the rear fenders. The fenders themselves have been bobbed slightly.

A series of more subtle body changes round out the car. Things like missing drip rails, a flush-mount windshield and re-formed sheet metal above the windshield. The simple dashboard with its five

Rivaling the front for sparkle and sophistication, the rear suspension is based on a Corvette center section. Axle *shafts are tapered, hubs and everything else are polished, JFZ brake calipers are mounted inboard.*

Dashboard of Fred's car uses round, analog gauges. Seats, door panels and headliner are the work of Larry Sneed.

gauges was built in Boyd's shop, while the interior was stitched up by Larry Sneed of Louisville, Kentucky. The Ford bucket seats as well as the door panels are covered by Mercedes tan cloth with leather inserts.

Lest anyone suggest that this beauty is meant for show only, considerable time and effort went into the "go" part of the equation. It's a small-block yes, but a small-block with a difference. A combination of a Crower stroker crank and Venolia pistons gives a displacement of 383 ci. The aluminum heads were manufactured by Brownfield and carry Chevrolet 2.02 in. intake valves and polished ports. A roller cam and roller rockers make the valves go up and down, while a set of Weber carbs provide the gas and air.

Since buying the car, Fred has been chosen for Boyd's Pro Pick at the Goodguys event and Top 25 at Pigeon Forge. The road was long, but the trip was worth it. After starting on one Vicky, Fred now owns another. Not exactly the car he started out to build—but considering who built the car and how well it turned out, that might be all for the best.

The small-block in Fred's car has been leaned on: Venolia pistons, Crower rods and crank give a total displacement of 383 ci. Brownfield aluminum heads are equipped with roller rockers. Carburetion is by Weber. Fred reports that when he pushes on the loud pedal, the results are both instantaneous and dramatic.

Next page
Fred Warren stands with his Boyd Coddington-built Vicky. Fred owns a number of street rods including a rare Deuce sedan delivery.

My Deuce at My Price

Building by Barter

It all started when Roger Ward saw this Deuce roadster body and chassis sitting in Alan Grove's shop south of Kansas City. Roger was in the mood for a new ride and he'd always had a soft spot for '32 roadsters. There was only one problem. As Roger tells it: "Alan wanted ten grand for the body and chassis, and I just didn't have ten grand."

The answer to the problem came in the form of a conversation with Curt Cunningham from Carriage Works. Roger explained that he wanted to build a Deuce on a budget—and Curt suggested a swap. Curt offered to build a nice Carriage Works chassis if Roger (well known within the street rod industry for his paint work) would paint a Vicky street rod Curt had in the shop. This swap with Curt was the first, though not the final, labor-for-labor trade Roger used to get his Deuce at his price.

Curt started with two frame rails from a company known as Just A Hobby. The frame rails

were tied together with Carriage Works cross-members. Roger likes his cars real, real low, so Curt used a Magnum front axle with a 4 in. drop. Holding it all up is a front spring from Posies while the four-bar system from Carriage Works keeps it all in place. The front spindles too are from Magnum, while the front rotors and calipers are from the Wilwood company. Steering is done through a Vega gear connected cross-steer style to the right spindle assembly. In the rear Curt used the street rodder's favorite: a 9 in. Ford rear end suspended by a triangulated four-bar system and Spax coil-over shocks.

The chassis was nearly completed when Curt became just too busy to finish it, so Roger took it first to Pete and Jake's and then to Alan Grove to wrap up all the details. Yes, Alan Grove got some nice graphics painted on his shop truck in payment for his metal work.

Swapping is great for the budget, but of course there is a hidden cost. That cost is extra time; it seems that everything takes a little longer under the barter system. When Roger started on the roadster he thought in terms of the then-current smooth look. By the time he was actually ready to mount the Wescott body and buy the accessories, he could see the trends starting to change. He also realized that even with the trading, the car would be more expensive than any of his other street rods—so maybe he should try and build a timeless design that would still look good in five or ten years.

Instead of high-tech and ultra-smooth, Roger chose a vintage theme with modern accents. The real key to the vintage look is the Du Vall windshield

A combination of old and new, Roger Ward's roadster includes a variety of styling cues. Du Vall windshield, solid wheels and large-diameter lights are all throwbacks to the early fifties. More modern are the missing door handles and hinges, and the nearly monochromatic paint scheme.

The real key to the vintage look is the Du Vall windshield installed on the Deuce cowl

installed on the Deuce cowl. Mounted at a rather steep angle, the split windshield brings back images of early hot rods from the late forties and early fifties.

Reinforcing the vintage feel are the large-diameter headlights from Vintique. Rather than create a complete nostalgia rod, Roger chose to use solid hood sides, built by Curt Cunningham, and a subtle beige paint job without any striping.

For a top, Roger wanted something with the right look that could be easily lifted on and off. First, he created the right shape with a framework

Interior too is old and new: Leather-covered seats and door panels seem high-tech. Spoked steering wheel and classic, black-on-white gauges look like something from an early issue of Hop Up magazine.

Grille insert is a classic design done in stainless. Front axle is from Magnum, dropped 4 in. and painted body color. Front disc brake rotors and calipers are from Wilwood.

Through hard work and imagination, Roger and friends have created a Deuce that defies attempts to place it in any one niche

of carefully bent electrical conduit. Next, the areas between the tubing were filled with sheet aluminum. Finally, the finished framework would be padded and covered when the car was upholstered. The finished top is attached with six bolts and weighs only 40 lbs.

The engine under Roger's smooth, three-piece hood definitely falls into the modern category. John Barrett assembled the small-block with balanced internals, ported heads and a 601 camshaft from Crane. Sitting on top is a 750 cfm Carter carburetor feeding a B&M blower. The combination of huffer and healthy small-block is good for 460 hp at 6000 rpm—not bad for a 2,350 lb. car.

As the car finally started to come together there were all the little things to take care of: The stainless-steel exhaust system, consisting of Sanderson headers and custom exhaust pipes and mufflers, was built by Don Cain. The stainless-steel brake lines were laid out by Leon Holman. And

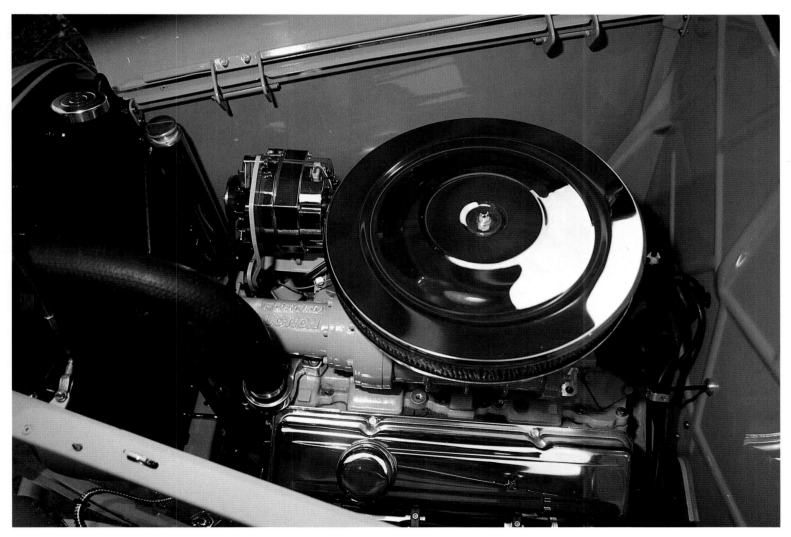

Taillights are the standard-issue '39 Ford lights. Instead of frenching them into the body, Roger built slightly raised platforms as the mounting surface. The effect makes the lights look as though they were built for this body.

Born to boogie—Roger Ward's 350 Chevrolet gets its fuel and air from a Carter four-barrel feeding a B&M blower. All internals have been balanced; camshaft is a 601 model from Crane.

finally, the dashboard of black anodized aluminum with VDO Classic gauges was built by G. W. Taylor.

After nearly three years of waiting, Roger's roadster was almost done. The only thing left was a trip from Ottawa, Kansas, to Durant, Iowa—home of Steve and Marilyn Ralfs' small upholstery shop. While most businesses work at getting bigger, Steve and Marilyn work at staying small. They work on only one car at a time—that way one car will never act as the layout table for another. Steve custom-built the bucket seats so Marilyn could cover them, then went on to fabricate and cover the door panels. The upholstery is leather while the carpets are a synthetic material designed to look like wool, but better able to withstand that occasional downpour.

Most Deuces fall into one of two categories: either retro rod or high tech. With a Flathead and external hinges they become nostalgia pieces. Install a small-block and knock off the hinges and you've got a modern smoothie. Through hard work and imagination, Roger and friends have created a Deuce that defies attempts to place it in any one niche. A unique Deuce at a reasonable price—quite an accomplishment any way you look at it.

Roger Ward is well known among the street rodding community for his fine paint work. The roadster is a car Roger had wanted to build for many years.

Details of perfection. The headlight, steering and front suspension components on Roger Ward's Deuce roadster combine function with form.

113

Two That Henry Forgot to Build

Moving the Deuce into the 1990s

A great design begins with a talented designer. Though the individual who penned the original Deuce has been lost to history—most think it was Edsel—the designer responsible for these two radical Deuces is Thom Taylor. Thom is responsible for many award-winning street rods, cars produced by the likes of Boyd Coddington and Ken Fenical, owner of the street rod shop known as Posies.

Thom admits to a special fondness for '32 Fords: "The Deuce has always been one of my favorites. I did these newer, unusual designs because I got tired of people saying that the '32 was boring, that it had been 'done to death,' and that there wasn't anything new that could be done to a '32 Ford. I see all these people moving toward newer cars and I thought that maybe some new ideas would help to keep them interested in the Deuce. I also tried to design cars that retained the best of the original design—cars that are unmistakably Deuces."

In early 1988, *Street Rodder* ran a series of Thom's '32 Ford renderings. One of the drawings was a two-door Deuce with a canvas top, and the other was a more radical fastback design. The drawings struck the fancy of a certain well-known East Coast street rod builder, Ken Fenical from Posies. Following a phone conversation between Ken and Thom, more drawings were mailed to the Posies shop in Hummelstown, Pennsylvania. Shortly after receiving the sketches, Ken promised to produce both cars, one in 1989 and one in 1990.

The canvas-topped Club Sport coupe would be first, followed by the Speed-Back coupe. Both would be built in the Posies shop using straightforward street rod chassis. And both would be built to make a statement about Posies—about the shop's commitment to building creative cars that spawn controversy and, hopefully, more creativity in the street rod industry.

Club Sport Coupe

The canvas-topped coupe with the wild graphics started as a Downs Manufacturing three-window coupe. Creating the car seen in Thom's sketches took more than just a new canvas top, though. Major body modifications include: a cowl and windshield frame from a cabriolet; modified doors with the rear post slanted forward; and a modified rear deck so a rear seat could be included in the design. Finally, after all the other work had been done, a new canvas top could be stretched over a series of bows.

The convertible top was created to look like a convertible—not a Carson top. It looks so genuine that people have asked Ken to lower the lid. There's

Two unique, modern Deuces from the Posies shop in Hummelstown, Pennsylvania. Posies owner Ken Fenical likes to build cars that ignite controversy and make people think. Both cars originated in the fertile imagination of Thom Taylor.

The Club Sport coupe, rear, was the first of the two cars to be built. Though it looks like a true convertible, the top is on to stay. Note the change in the angle of the door post. More radical than the Club Sport coupe, the Speed-Back, front, is based on a rendering by Thom Taylor. Front frame rails have been kicked to get the car low; front fenders sit higher in relation to the hood than stock.

Next page
Though Henry Ford built a Sport coupe in 1932, it lacked the nice flowing lines of this one. Roofline comes back quite far before meeting the trunk. Larger cabin includes room for a back seat.

only one problem, the top doesn't go down. Ken believes that while convertibles look great, most lose those great looks once the top comes down. And since this Deuce was built for visual appeal, well then there's no point in putting the top down.

The more subtle body changes were initiated by the Posies shop after they received the renderings from Thom. Like the bobbed rear fenders and the small nerf-bar bumpers done at the new owner's

request. At the front of the coupe the radiator has been moved forward almost 2 in., while the front gravel pan and fenders have been molded together. The front turn signals are mounted behind small, oval perforations in the front fenders.

The new radiator position required a new hood and side panels, fabricated in the Posies shop. At the same time the boys in the shop created a new mounting and hinging system. The convertible-

116

Wood inlays are real ash burl cut and fit by Don Stevens, the coupe's owner. The rest of the interior was stitched up in the Posies shop.

coupe's hood top lifts up and forward and the solid side panels come off in less than one minute, providing quick and complete access to the engine.

The wild graphics that cover the car were designed by the crew at Posies, working from sketches sent by Thom. Both the yellow cream base paint and the aqua graphics were painted in the paint booth at Posies.

Posies is a one-stop-shop kind of street rod emporium. Among the many services offered is complete trim and interior work. The dashboard in the coupe is a collaboration between Posies and the coupe's owner, Don Stevens. Don is a wood craftsman by trade, so it's not too surprising that the custom dashboard uses more than just wood veneer.

The two dash panels are covered with real inserts of ash burl, cut and finished by Don. The wood was chosen both for its pattern and its color, so as to blend better with the colors used both inside and outside the car. In the center of the dash sit the necessary gauges; on the lower panel are the air conditioning vents and the radio. The wood theme has been carried through to the wooden inserts in the door panels and the woodgrain steering wheel. The rest of the interior was done by Posies. The colors are beige and light brown. The effect is tasteful, comfortable and restrained.

Under all the high-tech fiberglass is a rather normal street rod chassis. The rails are from Just A Hobby, with cross-members built in the Posies shop. At the front a dropped axle is supported by a Posies

Radiator has been moved forward to accommodate the longer 351 ci Ford V-8.

Super-Slide spring and a Pete & Jakes four-bar setup. The rear suspension relies on two more Super-Slide springs mounting a Ford 8 in. rear axle.

Motive power for Don's Club Coupe comes from a Ford 351 ci Windsor engine coupled to a C-4 automatic transmission. Pete Mitten of Newville, Pennsylvania, massaged the 351 with a Crane cam, Edelbrock Torquer manifold and Holley four-barrel carburetor.

Speed-Back Coupe

Though both of the Thom Taylor designs show a certain restraint, and both keep the necessary Deuce signatures, the metallic aqua Speed-Back seems the more radical of the two concepts. The new roofline and rounded door cuts—combined with creative touches performed by Posies—all serve to set this one car apart from any other.

The Speed-Back started out as another Downs three-window coupe body. When Ken started on the project, he swore the finished car would contain a minimum of the standard street rod accessories. Ken saw Thom's renderings as a starting point for a great car. He felt that by combining the talents of Thom Taylor with those of the Posies crew, an outstanding street rod would result.

The largest part of the new car's creation would be the top. Thom Taylor came to Posies to help transform those lines of the drawing into the actual shape done in fiberglass. First they cut off the old top, leaving the windshield posts and frame. Then a large piece of foam was dropped on top where the roof used to be. Thom spent eight hours working on

The side-mount spare gives the car a feeling of class, as though it might be a classic Packard or Lincoln

one side of the foam, creating the right shape. Once one side was finished, it took only four hours to duplicate those lines on the other side of the car.

Once Thom had carved the correct fastback shape, the foam block was covered with the fiberglass fabric and resins that would eventually form the new top. When the fiberglass was rigid enough, the whole affair was lifted off the car so the foam plug could be popped out. Presto, one new fiberglass, fastback top. Eventually the top was reinforced with additional layers of fiberglass and a metal framework, and grafted back onto the body.

The other major change to the glass Deuce body and the other part of Thom's original design

Headlights are mounted directly to the fender. Small turn signals cut right into the fender lip are rather ingenious.

120

Ken Fenical bought some unusual rearview mirrors for the car—and liked their shape so well he bought two more and converted them to taillight housings.

involved the wonderful rounded door cuts. They somehow work in harmony with both the fadeaway top and the lines of the rear deck lid and trunk.

Mounted on the right running board is the solo, side-mount spare tire. Though offered as an option on Henry's cars, they were seldom seen then and are almost never seen now. The side-mount spare gives the car a feeling of class, as though it might be a classic Packard or Lincoln.

Previous page
The unusual profile is created by fastback roof design and laid-back windshield posts. Front fenders have been moved up, rear fenders have been bobbed.

As promised when Ken started the project, the outside bits and pieces—designed and created by Posies—are every bit as unique as the top. The bumpers are hollow, each one created by welding two '40 Ford bumpers together to make the smooth, strong shapes. The headlights are Model A driving lights; the taillight housings started out as rearview mirrors. After buying the mirrors, Ken liked the shape so much he bought two more and turned them into taillight assemblies.

The interior of Ken's latest project was inspired by the new Mercedes roadster. Built in the Posies shop, the interior and dashboard were of an

Side-mount spare gives the car a feeling of class, as though it might be a coach-built Packard or Duesenberg. Rounded door cuts work in harmony with the roof and

trunk line. Bumpers are '40 Ford units, two on each end welded together to form a strong, tubular bumper.

interesting asymmetric design. The steering wheel and instruments from a Ford truck are part of a housing that sits way over on the driver's side. Across the rest of the dash there is only padded white vinyl and the black air conditioning outlets. Around the perimeter of the mostly white interior is a contrasting black belt that serves to tie everything together.

The specs for the chassis of this New-Edge (Ken's term for Posies' new 1990s style street rod

projects) Deuce read much like those of the Sport Club coupe. The frame is made up of Just A Hobby rails combined with Posies' own cross-members. Getting the nose in the weeds was accomplished by kicking the frame 2½ in. in front, which meant the front fenders had to be moved up as well. Front suspension is by dropped tube axle, a Posies Super-Slide spring and a Pete and Jake's four-bar system. In the rear, the Ford 8 in. axle is suspended by a set of coil-overs and a Pete and Jake's four-bar system.

Perhaps more important, he and Thom have shown us that there's always something new to do—if we can only break away from doing what everyone else is doing

The engine in Ken's newest creation is a brand-new Chevrolet High Output V-8. The small-block is mostly stock, with the stock Chevrolet camshaft and heads. Sitting on top is a Carter four-barrel carburetor and a customized B&M air cleaner. The Chevy motor passes its power through a rebuilt 350 Turbo transmission.

Pointing the Way—the Future of Deuces

One of Ken's stated goals when he took on the two Taylor-inspired projects was to create a catalyst to bring about more creativity in the street rod industry. Looking at the two coupes, that seems to be the most simple of his contributions. Perhaps more important, he and Thom have shown us that there's always something new to do—if we can only break away from doing what everyone else is doing.

By building two Deuces with just enough of the old to go with the new, they have also shown us the way to the future. A future where '32 Fords are still considered viable designs and desirable street rods.

Interior is just as unique as the exterior. Dash pod is from a Ford truck. White vinyl seats and door panels were done in the Posies shop.

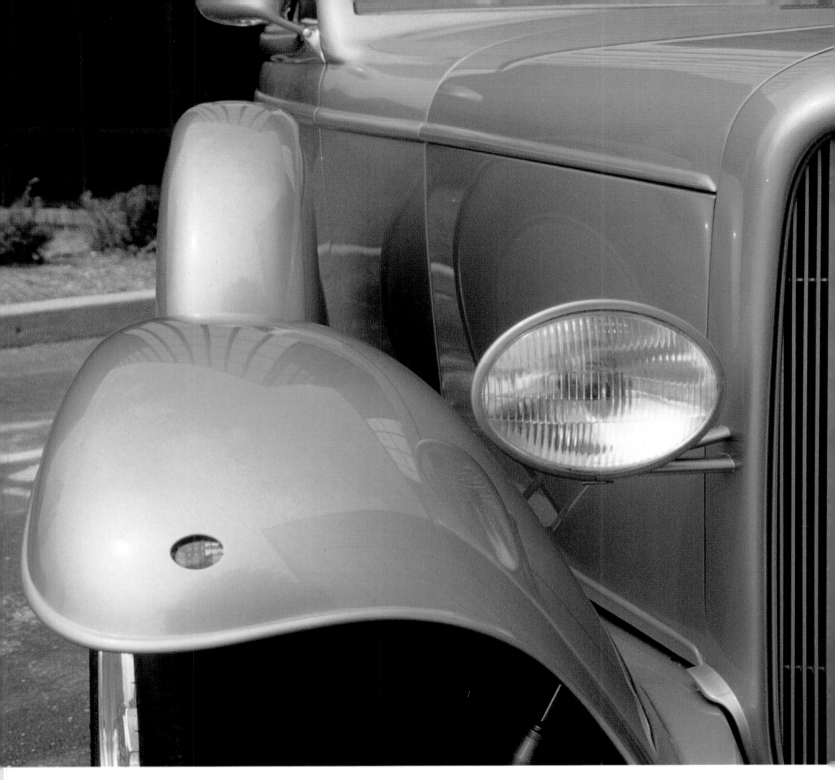

Ellipsoid headlights were originally Model A driving lights. Small turn signal is cut out in the same oval shape.

Next page
Unusual roof was formed from a large block of foam. When the shape was right, the foam became a form around which the new glass top could be laid up.

Index